Pragmalytics

Pragmalytics

Practical Approaches to Marketing Analytics in the Digital Age

CESAR A. BREA

iUniverse, Inc.
Bloomington

Pragmalytics
Practical Approaches to Marketing Analytics in the Digital Age

iUniverse books may be ordered through booksellers or by contacting:

iUniverse
1663 Liberty Drive
Bloomington, IN 47403
www.iuniverse.com
1-800-Authors (1-800-288-4677)

ISBN: 978-1-4759-5956-7 (sc)
ISBN: 978-1-4759-5008-3 (ebk)

Printed in the United States of America

iUniverse rev. date: 12/10/2012

The promise of marketing analytics in the age of Big Data is the ability to make your marketing efforts much more targetable, trackable, and testable. But in practice, realizing this promise is hard—logically, technically, and especially organizationally.

Pragmalytics helps you address this challenge with practical techniques and real-world examples, to help you better navigate the modern marketing forest among ever-denser thickets of data, channels, and tools.

CONTENTS

PART III: The Human Dimension

ACKNOWLEDGEMENTS

Many people encouraged me through this project and helped me to improve the result. Among them, special thanks go to Mike Bernstein, Tip Clifton, Susan Ellerin, Ann Hackett, Perry Hewitt, Jeff Hupe, Ben Kline, Janelle Leonard, Bob Neuhaus, Judah Phillips, Trish Rogers, Rob Schmults, Michelle Seaton, Tad Staley, and my business partner Jamie Schein for challenging and encouraging me. If you like any of this, they get credit for salvaging it. The rest is my responsibility.

I'd also like to thank the wonderful clients and colleagues I've had the opportunity to work with and learn from. And, of course, I appreciate very much the patience and support I received from my family, especially from Nan, Ben, Kate, and Will, to whom this is dedicated.

Dover, Massachusetts

March 2012

INTRODUCTION

Over the last ten years, as more and more marketing attention and dollars have been allocated to digital channels, we've all been in meetings that play out a distressingly similar conflict. On one side are men and women from Mars: left-brained, analytical to a fault, and devoted to the power of the data they have collected. On the other are the folks from Venus: right-brained, fiercely proud of their creativity, and jealously protective of both the brand and the customer experience. Stuck in the middle are the people of Earth, the executives charged with using a limited budget to hit a defined target on a short deadline.

From what I've seen, the best decisions to emerge from these meetings never come from executives who reject data and competent analysis in favor of intuition. Nor does a blind faith in data warehouses and mix models alone point the way toward sunlit uplands of growth and profitability. The best solutions come from a practical, transparent push-and-pull between these points of view, as long as the people involved do three things: They must present well-informed positions; they must communicate these positions clearly; and they must be committed to the process of making a good-enough decision on a timely basis to allow for competent execution.

I grew up professionally in environments that preached data-supported decision-making, and I'm very excited about the new analytic possibilities, particularly by their potential to overcome important cognitive biases.[1]

Four years ago, I left a perfectly good job to start Force Five Partners to help clients take better advantage of these possibilities.

What did my co-founder Jamie Schein and I see that informed our approach to analytics? We have spent 20 years at the intersection of marketing and high technology as executives, entrepreneurs, and advisors. Collectively, we've worked with more than 50 different firms in a dozen different sectors, including leading brands in retail, media, telecommunications, financial services, education, and health care. We've seen a lot of what we call "supply-side evangelism," meaning a devotion to the latest new channels of information and a parochial advocacy for the Big Data these channels churn out. Maybe as a consequence of this evangelism, we have also observed a lot of demand-side skepticism, and also paralysis in the face of this growing mountain of data.

Realizing the potential of marketing analytics means looking beyond the smart people and their cool tools. It means helping senior teams align and focus on questions worth asking. It means organizing the data so that you can more easily access it. It means building flexibility into your processes and underlying operational infrastructure, so that your organization can act more easily on data-related insights. Frequently, it also means teaching team members to embrace the data rather than to fight or ignore it. To do that, you need to cultivate an "analytic marketer" mindset at both the individual and organizational level so that team members, even those outside the marketing department, can use your insight to inform important decisions.

Our firm grew out of a desire to help organizations find these "pragmatically analytic" approaches to data-driven decision-making. This book synthesizes our experiences in doing so, and explains how we do what we do for our clients.

---

[1]   The "List of Cognitive Biases" found on Wikipedia may be worth reading, http://bit.ly/lUo46C.

This Book Is For You If:

- You are a general manager, or a senior sales or marketing executive.
- You are 10 percent behind plan or need to figure out how to hit a 10 percent growth target with little or no incremental budget, thanks to the current economic realities.
- You are pushing more and more of your chips into digital channels, some of which are so new that you can barely understand them (as they can barely explain themselves).
- Your head is spinning from the complexity of managing all of these channels—web activity, display ads, organic and paid searches, affiliate rewards, campaigns involving email, mobile devices, and social media. And you still have to manage print, TV, radio, and outdoor ads. Plus, you must convert effectively in your websites, call centers and stores.
- You have smart folks both inside and outside the firm working for you in each of these channels, but the marginal returns on dollars put into each of them have begun to level off.
- You feel that the Big Data these channels pump out should be a godsend, giving you the ability to target, track and test these marketing efforts, making them much more efficient and effective. Instead, these channels have become a data management and reporting nightmare for you. They generate confusion instead of insights.
- You continue to read and hear about cutting-edge marketing gurus and their analytic high priests applying complex tools and models to interpret and predict customer behavior.
- You believe in using marketing data as a tool, and yet you're concerned about over-engineering solutions to overly narrow problems.
- Your biggest questions are utterly practical in nature: How to identify and address the bottlenecks in the budget; where to shift the money to close that 10 percent gap; and where that money will come from.
- You need to know how to minimize the risks for the investments you need to make.

- You want to know how to communicate an understanding of analytics in a way that everyone, within and beyond marketing, can understand and use this data to solve organizational problems.
- You want to know how to develop an organization that can take advantage of analytics.

Scope and Purpose

The Pragmalytics philosophy is applicable across the broad spectrum of analytics, in the marketing domain and beyond. However, this book would collapse under its own weight if it tried to explain how to apply these ideas universally.

So, we need to focus. The biggest opportunities in marketing today lie in integrating channels so that they provide consistent and efficient customer experiences, and then targeting these experiences to the right customers. However, you can still drown in data while trying to do this. You can also trigger multiple organizational problems, particularly if you tackle this effort as a capability-building initiative per se, rather than using it to identify and solve specific problems. (Remember that you can always generalize solutions afterward.)

The main purpose of this book is to offer you specific tools, techniques, and ideas to help you analyze your organizations' marketing efforts so that you can make better, timelier decisions about what to keep, change, drop, and add to the marketing experiences you're trying to create.

ROI

At Force Five Partners, we have found that we can identify, and under the right conditions, achieve at least a 25 percent improvement in a variety of factors, including sales. We can get these results significantly faster, and using far fewer resources across the scope of the business in which you apply these ideas. For example, in some of our most recent work with a complex, multi-channel firm, we have seen a doubling of lead and conversion rates in a critical seasonal campaign.

Beyond this, the approach creates a smoother, more consistent process for making marketing decisions. It allows people involved in these decisions a few extra cycles to try to see further ahead, and crucially, a few more experience-building "reps" to build mastery.

Where This Book Fits

This book isn't Marketing or Stats 101. It assumes that you know how to manage costs on the basis of clicks (CPC) and impressions (CPM) and that models and tests are sometimes part of how you try to steer ahead. This book describes how to create the conditions for analytic success and then fulfill that potential.

Also, I assume that you are familiar with popular zeitgeist titles about the possibilities inherent in data mining, titles such as *Supercrunchers* by Ian Ayres, and *Competing on Analytics* by Tom Davenport and Jeanne Harris. Both of these explore the big picture possibilities in large-scale data analysis. You may also have read or heard about the excellent subject matter resources such as *Web Analytics* and *Web Analytics 2.0* by Avinash Kaushik as well as *Web Analytics Demystified* by Eric Petersen. These books detail analytic theory and practical experience for those who have day-to-day contact with raw marketing data that emerges from different channels, and need to make something of it and communicate it effectively.

I've written Pragmalytics as a bridge between these two realms, the world of big picture promise and the real world of data harvesting. My goal is to help senior executives pay off on the promise of Big Data and use it to drive sustained bottom-line success in their businesses. So once again, this is a book for senior executives who develop the overall marketing plan of their organizations, and who are responsible for creating and sustaining the conditions for success we describe.

How This Book Is Organized

This book addresses three dimensions of the overall challenge faced by today's marketers: logical, technical, and human. The first section addresses the logical dimension, and provides

- a framework for identifying needs and opportunities to change marketing targeting, mix, and execution;
- a simple construct for re-integrating and managing customer experiences;
- an approach for de-averaging the overall performance of your customer experience across customer segments you want to target, so you can figure out how to adjust experience elements and target these adjustments appropriately;
- a collection of specific analytic techniques and heuristics designed to keep your team thinking and acting, as one senior executive said wistfully to me, "more like decision-makers and less like accountants."

The second section tackles the technical side and deals in particular with data challenges. Specifically, it suggests

- ideas for how you can string together data from different channels to appropriately personalize an experience, make it seamless, and further illuminate your understanding of customer habits, to anticipate and respond to customers' future needs; and,
- a lightweight set of requirements that forms a kind of scaffolding for data in order to provide analytic support for marketing decisions.

The third section addresses the personal and organizational terrain of marketing analytics, with ideas for

- how to recruit and develop a team of pragmalytic marketers; and
- how to build bridges across the organization to get the data you need and to more effectively communicate and implement the decisions you make.

A Work In Progress

This book has many areas of wet cement, which is appropriate in a field that is evolving at such an astonishing pace. If you have questions more specific to your situation, or about material not covered in this book, I hope to hear from you. My hope is to create a series on the issues covered here that includes your experiences and successes. Please drop me a note: cbrea@forcefivepartners.com.

PART I

The Logical Dimension

ONE

The Analytic Brief:
A Simple Organizing Framework

Marketing campaigns use creative briefs to outline insights about the target audience, the campaign objectives and its messages. Alongside these briefs come budgets and deadlines. What these documents rarely consider is how these campaigns will be measured, analyzed, and adjusted.

Yet the environment into which we launch and run these campaigns has changed. Channels have proliferated and evolve constantly. Audiences have fragmented, and individuals are influenced from a wider array of sources. Campaign success now depends on integrating campaign elements into programs that map to customers' multi-channel experiences. These programs must adapt frequently to rapid changes in these experiences, and they must be tailored appropriately to the needs of ever more fickle customers. The age of Big Ideas based on immediately obsolete concepts about these customers has passed.

Unfortunately, many organizations have become Balkanized by the specialized knowledge required to execute campaign elements in different channels. Marketing analytics efforts commissioned under these conditions often end up as islands of optimization that under-achieve their promise because they have not been framed in a way that allows others to understand what they do, and why.

At Force Five Partners, we have built and applied a framework for marketing analytics that complements a campaign's creative brief. We call it the Analytic Brief. Its role is to provide a common language that explains why various analytic efforts are needed and how they will work.

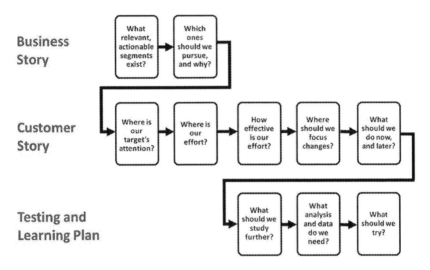

Figure 1: The Analytic Brief

The Analytic Brief has three main components: a Business Story, a Customer Story, and a Testing and Learning Plan. Each of these components includes a set of simple questions. Together, these buckets and associated questions help to focus conversations about marketing analysis and campaigns.

The Analytic Brief structure is intentionally simple. A shared understanding and well-integrated execution rarely follow from dueling broadsides of 75-page PowerPoint decks. In reality, marketing programs are a complex collection of wiggling, squirming variables. People meeting to decide and coordinate their efforts need an independent, common structure on which to pin these variables, so that everyone can evaluate them critically. Put another way, when you're deep in some multivariate jungle, whacking away at a thicket of channel attribution co-variances with the dull machete of barely-remembered concepts from Stats 101, it helps to have GPS and a mapping app on your smartphone. The Analytic Brief has filled this need effectively for us.

The **Business Story** asks you to describe and explain your choices about the customers you seek in any given marketing effort. It asks two straightforward questions.

1. Which relevant, actionable marketing segments exist?
2. Which ones should we pursue, and why?

While it may seem absurdly obvious to address this, I've found that many times marketing teams fail to ask and answer these essential questions. It's not that they don't think identifying customer segments is important. Rather, their plans fail to offer explicit and consistent details about the customer and about how the marketing program will map to her needs. Also, the terms *relevant* and *actionable* are critical. Many times, a plan will refer to market segmentation that includes dimensions relevant to product design or pricing, for example, but that don't consider channel design. Even when these plans do consider channel design, such as distinguishing between traditional customers and those who are digitally savvy, these segments may not be drawn in ways that allow us to identify or reach such people.

Once you have settled on customers to target, you can focus on the **Customer Story**. Here you answer five questions.

1. Where is our target's attention?
2. Where is our effort?
3. How effective is our effort?
4. Where should we focus our changes?
5. What should we do now, versus later?

These questions force you to approach any proposed campaign and associated analysis from a customer's perspective. Just as the Business Story helps to remind you which customers are the objects of your affection and why, the Customer Story explains why you're sitting through a discussion about, say, improving the usability of your mobile app. Look again at the final question. What should we do now versus later? This serves as a reminder that the customer experience bottleneck is constantly shifting. Remember that improvement efforts aimed at those bottlenecks need to show rapid response. A perfect but delayed improvement is worse than a rapid improvement that is merely good enough.

The **Testing and Learning Plan** reinforces this emphasis on focus and practicality. It asks just three questions.

1. What should we study further?
2. What data and analysis do we need?
3. What should we try?

The first question focuses scarce analytic resources on questions where the stakes and uncertainty are high. The second question demands an outside-in approach. Consider what you need to get and do in order to arrive at an acceptably rigorous answer given the stakes and the uncertainty involved. Many people look at the data they have and the default analytic standards your team has been trained to use. Focus on what data you need in order to make a decision rather than on what data you happen to have. The final question asks you to consider taking a risk. Not everything should be modeled to death. Sometimes it's far better to get into the market with a thoughtful test of an idea for improving performance, rather than guessing at how customers might react with an analysis that is inherently rear-view.

I've used the Analytic Brief in multiple ways. Of course, I use it primarily as a framework for planning and evaluating marketing programs. It also works well as a guide for facilitating meetings. For example, when folks disagree on something, the brief enables us to identify and isolate the specific reasons for that disagreement. The brief also works as a broader capability-building checklist, based on how well an individual team is able to answer these questions. And it can serve as a precursor to IT specifications, training programs, hiring plans, and job specs. Through it all, you are using alignment as the common denominator for applying it effectively.

TWO

Re-Integrating Experiences

We've all heard the time-worn advice to look at the world from a customer's point of view. Yet this advice is still mostly observed in the breach. For example, many retailers still manage in-store and ecommerce channels as separate businesses that communicate under bi-lateral trade agreements, even though most customers wish to use these channels as complements rather than substitutes. This practice may be a legacy of the past or a reflection of present rivalries. In each of these cases, the structure of the business serves the past or the competition between managers rather than the customer.

When this basic structural myopia exists, it repeats itself on every level of the business. Individual components of the offline and online experiences get improved as locally optimized projects, wholly disconnected from a larger frame of reference. Managers elect to optimize the experience of the customer only with regard to their channel. They easily forget that a customer who purchases a product in-store may wish to obtain a refund or fill out a survey or change a delivery date online. When customers can't do that, they get upset.

How do you re-integrate these channels into one seamless business? How do you get everyone on board with this idea? The answer lies in building an ideal target customer experience as the foundation for your marketing analytics efforts and then optimizing your investments based on how well they influence this experience.

Briefly About Segments

While segmentation should always be the point of departure for any marketing campaign, there's no need to detail a plan for segmentation here. Rather than summarize all that has been written about segmentation, I'd like to focus on two keys to successfully defining a customer segment for the purpose of the analytic brief.

1. The segmentation used must be relevant to the marketing decision being made. For example, taking a demographic approach may not be relevant to a question about whether or not to build a mobile app. Rather, you might try and distinguish between attitudes or behaviors that are relevant to mobile app usage.
2. The segmentation must have markers that allow you to find and identify the customers you want. Such markers might be characteristics, behaviors, or attitudes that can be captured through surveys, or reliable proxies for behaviors or attitudes. For example, how many of your social media followers (and which ones) are posting from mobile devices? Your web analytics application can distinguish mobile browsers to tell you this.

A Customer Story for a Target Segment

Once you have a clear idea of which customer you'd like to target and why, you can start to think about the Customer Story.

When you design an experience, remember to focus on your target customer and his or her likely interactions with the business, often called a use case. Software designers refer to these profiles as functional specs. In the last ten years, the use of vivid user profiles, called personas, has become especially popular. These profiles were first described by Alan Cooper in his book *The Inmates Are Running The Asylum*. Since the publication of Cooper's book in 1998, the specifics of how to create a persona have wandered somewhat from his model. Creative briefs have also traditionally asked similar questions: "Who is the customer, and what are we trying to say to him or her, or get him or her to think, feel, and do?"

It is important is to describe dimensions of the target customer that are relevant not just to the product or service you're offering, but to the experience you want to support. For example, as discussed above, if using a mobile device is a core part of what you're describing, you might also cover a user's technical background and emotional relationship (e.g., status-seeking) with the device.

I have found it useful to use image-rich, narrated digital slideshows to detail a customer and experience story. This immersive format allows an audience to process the experience at both conscious and subliminal levels, which helps them absorb it better. It also makes their feedback more useful. You can always follow this presentation with the usual text or PowerPoint chaser that contains a complementary quantitative payload. (Ideally you have moved beyond static presentations of data to interactive displays,[2] but that's for another book.)

Mapping The Story

This right-brained story format must then be translated into a structure against which left-brained analytics can be applied. I've found it useful to create a visual map that shows how customers interact with different functions. I've used a variety of such matrix-based, ethnographic touchpoint mapping representations over the years. In the early 1990s, I learned business process re-engineering at Symmetrix, the firm created by Bain & Company co-founder George Bennett. More recently at Marketspace, Monitor Group's digital media and marketing practice, we applied another such view of buying process called Channel Pathways™. Harley Manning, vice president at Forrester Research, has described a similar approach. Akin Arikan and Don Peppers describe IBM's "Harvey Ball" and "Wiggly Line" charts in their excellent book, *Multichannel Marketing*. These are all

---

[2]   For example, http://www.tableausoftware.com/public/gallery/case-shiller-0

pretty basic but effective methods. In the last couple of years, we've settled on a single representation.

Start with a purchase funnel:

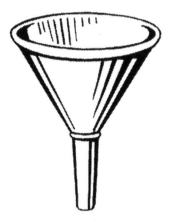

Figure 2: Purchase Funnel

Break out the purchase funnel into four simple stages:

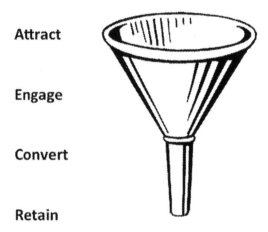

Attract

Engage

Convert

Retain

Figure 3: Purchase Funnel Generic Stages

Flip the funnel on its side to add a time dimension. Later this will give you some flexibility for scaling the relative length of different stages:

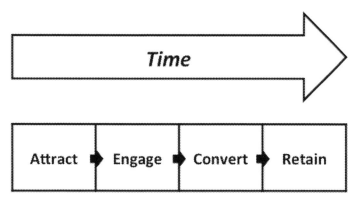

Figure 4: Buying Process

Array various relevant channels along a second dimension:

Purchase Process

Channels	Attract	Engage	Convert	Retain
Web Site				
Phone				
Search				
Display				
Facebook				
Television				
Stores				
Email				
Twitter				
Smartphone				
Blogs				
Affiliates				
Tablet				

Figure 5: Process/Channel Matrix

For each target customer segment, sketch a heat map identifying the primary and secondary channels that target customers use at each stage of the buying process:

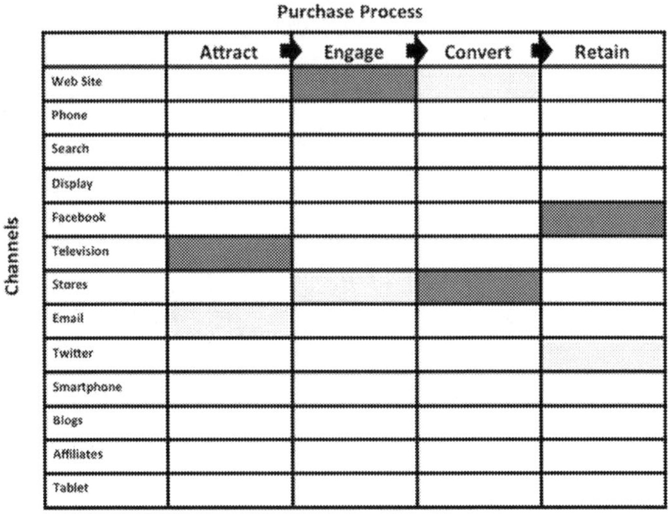

	Attract ➡	Engage ➡	Convert ➡	Retain
Web Site				
Phone				
Search				
Display				
Facebook				
Television				
Stores				
Email				
Twitter				
Smartphone				
Blogs				
Affiliates				
Tablet				

Purchase Process (columns) / *Channels* (rows)

Figure 6: Heat Map

For example, consider the chart above as it might relate to bachelors looking for sports cars. We know television dominates as the source for customer awareness of new models to consider. A bachelor who sees a commercial for a new model might go next to the manufacturer, a dealer, or third-party sites on the web to learn more about it. Finally, he makes his way to the dealership to shop and—ideally—to buy.

Of course, this bachelor might be a hipster or web nerd. He may see a tweet from a local dealer who services his old car, letting him know about new inventory. On his way home from work he might stop into the dealership (checking in on Foursquare, naturally) to have a look, maybe take a test drive. Finally, he might shop on the web to find the best price. On our chart, the final visit to the winning dealer is excluded from consideration because for this user it plays such a minimal role in the purchase decision.

We now have more hooks that help us track the customer experiences in order to attribute each channel's contribution to the final decision. For example, the URL used in the TV ad might be a deep link (e.g., luxuryautoco.com/newsportscar/) to a specially designed landing page that picks up on the themes of the initial TV ads. The landing page might also include a scheduling module so that our buyer can arrange a time to see or test-drive the car of his dreams. But more than that, this process allows the dealer to learn that his 11 o'clock appointment also indicated certain traits and concerns, either explicitly through information provided in setting up the appointment, or implicitly through browsing history that is captured by these sites.

The degree to which different customers separate themselves into distinct, non-overlapping preferred experiences could also be a clue to behaviorally defined segmentation, relevant to channel design (for example, "In-Persons," or "Online Exclusives"). For example, suppose you knew that all of the folks who start out on email and land on the specific pages designed for that channel exhibit longer and more sophisticated browsing habits as evidenced by the way they use applications on the site. Maybe you can even see off-site behavior by integrating ad network data. With this information, you might further engineer specific segment-appropriate journeys by sending certain customers down more customized, or individualized paths that could include different pages, phone calls, or even in-person visits. Here's a way to represent these journeys visually:

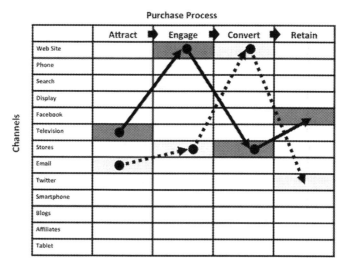

Figure 7: Segment-Specific Journeys

Evaluating Marketing in the Experience Context

Once you have described a target segment's experience in a fully integrated way, you can turn your attention to how well you currently fit to that experience.

When you ask the question about how much of the marketing budget should be put behind different channels or media, there are a number of impressive-sounding answers, including Channel Mix Optimization, Media Mix Modeling, and Media Planning. But life is rarely zero-based. So, perhaps a more pragmatic question is the one that asks how many resources should be moved and which channels should receive more or less emphasis.

There are many ways to answer this question. Some solutions are old and increasingly obsolete, while others are highly engineered, and a few are overly engineered. Somewhere along this spectrum is a solution that will prove best for you. This section suggests a way to find that happy medium. In particular, it will help you decide where you should focus your analytics and marketing automation investments.

The Old Way and the New Way

The Old Way of marketing considered that you had two main purposes and it asked to you invest in two kinds of communications. You bought television, radio, and print advertising to build your brand, and you used direct response channels to drive conversion. Old Way marketing decisions were brand-based. Episodic modeling efforts notwithstanding, these decisions were evaluated separately by individual channel and campaign. This evaluation was based mainly on one thing, brand lift, which was described by a subset of predictable values including awareness, favorability, preference, and intent. It was also evaluated by the efficiency with which you could achieve impressions goals, meaning reach and frequency, within your target audience. The Old Way relied on its own rules of thumb. For example, you might hear that you need three print impressions to get someone off the dime. (*Entrepreneur* has a good summary of the basics.[3] Also, SRDS Media Solutions provides some handy calculations.[4]) In Old Way direct marketing, it was typical for channels and campaigns to be evaluated on cost per lead (CPL) or cost per sale (CPS) basis.

This traditional approach has obvious limitations. It assumes that each channel functions independently of the others. The New Way integrates all the different types of messages and information flowing toward the customer, while tracking responses by the customer. It seeks to manage campaigns as consistent and coordinated executions that collectively support the experience we described earlier. For example the idea of attribution analysis has emerged as the next generation of media mix modeling. It helps marketers understand the contribution of interactions across the variety of channels along a customer's journey to the decision to purchase. Through attribution analysis, you can decide, for example, how much more or less investment to devote to paid search vs. email. Or you can determine which publishers in your display ad plan deserve more or less investment, or you can tune the trafficking rules for your participation in an ad network. Attribution analysis is very powerful, especially if you can establish a common currency for evaluating investments against each other.

As powerful as attribution analysis can be, it also can be extremely complicated to re-integrate customer experiences based on a fully attributed analysis of the impact of each channel. This is true even if you are looking only at the digital interactions.[5] This re-integration can also be hard to execute, particularly across online and offline channels, for a number of reasons. These reasons are not merely logical, but also technical, strategic, and organizational as well. More on that later.

One thing hasn't really changed much. As a practical matter, most marketing organizations and agencies are still divided into two camps: brand versus direct response. In each of these camps, digital channels and traditional channels compete for dollars and dominance. Nevertheless, the two are

---

[3] http://www.entrepreneur.com/encyclopedia/term/82454.html

[4] http://www.srds.com/frontMatter/sup_serv/calculator/index.html

[5] http://www.conversionworks.co.uk/blog/2009/06/11/super-cookie

managed separately for reasons that are as much about organization and culture as they are about the inability to integrate information.

Old Way marketers have long relied on some direct response techniques. For example, they have inserted unique phone numbers in the call-to-action parts of ads, so that they could track responses more tightly after an ad runs rather than looking simply at the timing of incoming phone calls. Similarly, unique catalog and discount codes have also long been used to identify sources. And, it is old hat to merge external and internal data to decide content and frequency offers and messages to send to different audiences.

The fragmentation of available media channels has changed everything. Customers can be engaged through email, text, multiple social media sites, personal accounts, loyalty cards, web searches, web ads with hypertext links, ads on smartphones, ads in online games. The list goes on and gets longer all the time. Each channel offers varying abilities to track potential customers. Each can be integrated to better coordinate your outreach to individual customers. The spectrum of possibilities has broadened, with each of the options along it providing a more limited, ephemeral reach.

And yet, many organizations stay stuck in the Old Way. Some are understandably overwhelmed by the choices that make the next step look like jumping straight to fifth gear. Others can't see how to embrace these options and still deliver enough reach. Many organizations end up marketing in more channels than they are capable of tracking well. This results in poor tracking within and across channels. Without good tracking, organizations have no idea which channels are providing a good return on invested resources. What's worse, these haphazard efforts provide a collectively disjointed experience for customers.

Moving Toward Marketing Mix Decisions

Let's return to our chart. To this point, we have described what your customers are up to. How do we evaluate your marketing strategy against that? As always, the first question to ask is, "How well do my activities and my investments match up to the heat map?"

Purchase Process

Channels	Attract ➡	Engage ➡	Convert ➡	Retain
Web Site	$$	$	$	
Phone				
Search				
Display				
Facebook				$
Television	$$			
Stores	$$$	$	$	
Email	$			
Twitter				$
Smartphone				
Blogs				
Affiliates				
Tablet				

Figure 8: Marketing Mix by Channel and Buying Stage

Obviously there are a variety of ways to draw these investment levels and to draw conclusions from them. One method is to look at spending on each channel relative to other expenditures, either as a whole or on a per unit basis. Another method is to look at expense in each on a per-customer basis. In this example, we might think about de-emphasizing store spending, and possibly beefing up email marketing.

Next you would want to ask, "What's the yield along the way?" There are several ways you can estimate this yield. You can measure the number of people who are engaged relative to the number who are attracted, and then measure the number who are converted relative to the number who are engaged. Or you can look directly at yields along journeys you define and track them using some of the techniques for linking and tracking experiences described above:

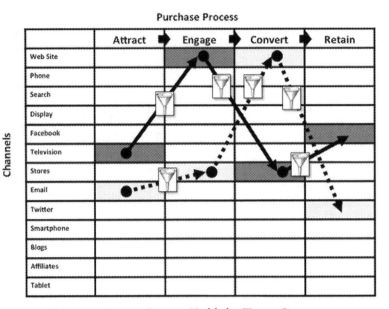

Figure 9: Buying Process Yields by Target Segment

The goal is to study the most dominant journey along the attract to retain pipeline, meaning the one used by your largest pool of potential customers, and to find in that journey the biggest breakdown, meaning the point at which you are leaking the most marginal profit contribution.

It seems so straightforward, unless you look at this journey and realize that yields are small everywhere. So, you ask, "How can I figure out which point should be my highest priority?" The good news is that it is easier today to assemble, for any given situation, multiple benchmarks from which you can interpolate an answer. For example, one good benchmark rule of thumb for a campaign is 2 to 3 percent of the initial touches. You can apply this benchmark to marketing touches for target customers not otherwise expressing any explicit or implicit purchase intent, all the way to purchase.

Some folks note that leading online retailers see conversion rates as high as ten times that 2 to 3 percent average.[6] And yet, this level of yield typically occurs when the site itself has been tuned purely for converting

---

[6]   http://www.clickz.com/3628276

well-qualified leads generated through an upstream ecosystem. Another benchmark asks you to look for a nearly 15 percent yield from attract to engage, and again from engage to convert, on a per-visit basis. With that benchmark in mind, you can try to optimize around the edges of these averages. You can do that by analyzing and experimenting to determine how to get more overall dollars through the pipeline, or you can try to add more audience in the earlier stages of the experience. You can achieve this either by spending more to broaden the targeting, or you can allocate more resources to try and engage and convert more of the traffic you already have. For the latter, you can use primary research via mystery shopping, focus groups, or surveys, and testing can be particularly useful in helping you decide where to allocate resources.

Different Approaches to Channel Impact Attribution

Once you've done a good job of linking channels both for the customer's experience and for your understanding, you'll want to figure out each channel's role in driving potential customers onward. However, this can get hairy because of the channel fragmentation noted above.

Old-style top-down media mix models were fine when options were few, and marketers could only make lumpy commitments for large fixed media over a long time periods. Examples include purchases such as seasonal television show sponsorship or ads in specified spaces or time slots. Typically, the yield from these purchases could only be measured at similarly fixed points in time.

Ad markets have become more like financial securities markets in that they feature lots of options, lots of short-term trading, and instant accountability. All of this makes the analytic challenge tougher. Here's a good question: When you increase one type of advertising effort, such as television, print, radio, display ads and social media spending, how does search engine referral volume change? Here's another good question: How does an increase in any of these advertising venues change social media buzz? Underneath each of these question is the Old Way bias that surely there is one site, one ad network, one MSA, one lever to pull to get the right payout. While it is fairly straightforward to model these relationships at aggregate levels, parsing them more finely to decide specifically where to invest money is far harder.

When something is harder to do, often it is also much more expensive and takes a long time. Of course it's possible that a lengthy expensive process may be just what you need. If you are driving a Ferrari 599GTO, then you need to drop a 600-horsepower engine under the hood. If you are driving anything less, that engine would be a wasted resource. When you tackle the task of channel attribution, think in terms of two possible approaches. There is the simple but feasible approach, and there is the high performance approach. But don't feel constrained by the approach the Big Data vendor is pitching. Choose an approach based on what you need to achieve.

Simple and Feasible Approach

If the business itself is smaller and more straightforward, meaning it employs fewer channels and relies on a less complex decision-making process, you can optimize channel mix by making some rough, simplifying assumptions. While it's true that stimulating and tracking pre-purchase customer engagement is all the rage these days, you don't need to be a slave to that data. Lee Bissonnette, Senior VP of E-Commerce at Loehmann's uses a simplifying assumption that works well for his organization's goals. "Bottom line, I will pay less for intermediary clicks but continue to pay strongly for first click and last click. The in-between clicks are like the jelly and peanut butter, essential to the transaction, but without the bread a messy handful that doesn't get eaten," says Bissonnette. Another simplifying assumption would be to limit your analysis to touchpoints that are highly trafficked. For example, many clients in B2B or in some complex B2C products such as financial services, may find that Facebook may not yet be as relevant as an influence mechanism.

High Performance Approach

If you have the data and analytic infrastructure along with the team to support it, you can develop a common currency that allows you to measure the ROI of different channels, and at different levels of granularity on an apples-to-apples basis. If you can hook up the data properly, you can nuance your answers as conditions change. And for extra credit, you can add the ability to ask, "What if?" With a lot of marketing dollars at stake, this might be very worthwhile.

Even if you do choose to pursue this approach, you should still begin by focusing narrowly, meaning you should attempt to optimize investments for a specific conversion event that is influenced by two to three channels at most. The best way to choose this conversion event is to focus on where in the customer's journey the yields are smallest or where you are most uncertain about why these yields are small. Once you have applied some insights and achieved positive results from them, you can and should advance to greater analytic complexity. If you forge ahead too quickly, you will get crushed by the data and all its variables, and you will get talked into using complex strategies that lack clear payoffs.

All of the preceding discussion has been based on the funnel model for marketing, which you may have heard is out of fashion in some circles. These days, people like to say that the funnel model for marketing is dead, that it is just too deterministic. In its place, these same people suggest a variety of alternatives. The most persuasive of these describe potential customers as being in various levels of relative attention to their various needs, and therefore more or less susceptible to what they call *activation* with respect to acting on these needs. I think this is a horrible term. It sounds too much like *The Manchurian Candidate*.

What's helpful about these models is that they suggest that at upper levels of the funnel you should think differently about how to support customers who are ready to act versus those who are still collecting information. As a practical matter, the funnel model is easily adapted to accommodate this, by splitting the "Attract" phase into the first two stages of the classic

"Awareness / Interest / Decision / Action" (AIDA) construct that's been around for a long time. (See "The Marketing Funnel Is A Brita Water Filter" http://www.octavianworld.org/octavianworld/2011/04/the-marketing-funnel-is-a-brita-water-filter.html)

A Framework Is Only As Useful As the Data to Fill It

Optimizing channel mix is easier if you have good answers to the questions posed by the Analytic Brief. At Force Five Partners, when we work with a new client, we ask a series of questions that encourage a client to talk about segmentation, marketing channels and what a client knows or believes about customer experience. There aren't right or wrong answers. Rather, the answers given help us to get a sense for how to help clients get started. It also lets us know how much work will be involved in getting to a meaningfully improved channel mix. When we listen to the answers to certain questions, we know the degree to which analysis can be quantified with confidence. In other words, we can grade an answer in three ways. If we consider the answer to be *good*, that means that we can tell the organization has put a lot of thought into this question before we posed it. The answer is detailed and represents a fair amount of research or consideration. If we label an answer as *OK*, that means that the organization is grappling with this question, but doing so imperfectly, either because the organization is relying on intuition or generalizations for the answer, or because the data for this answer is old. If the answer given is *weak*, that means that the organization may never have considered this question before, or that the answer given will require much more research and effort to make it useful in the context of analytics.

I'll include a sample question and answers in each of the three buckets here. For the full diagnostic questionnaire with answers, turn to the Appendix and look for the "Analytic Brief Questionnaire."

Example: Which customers or groups are you targeting?

Answer A: Segmentation either doesn't exist, or it exists but is documented only in research. (Weak)

Answer B: Segmentation is integrated into our marketing plan, with clear ties between segments and campaign elements. (OK)

Answer C: Segmentation is relevant and actionable for the marketing investment decision being made. It has also been integrated into reporting and analysis that is used to track and manage the marketing plan. (Good)

THREE

De-Averaging Performance

Analytic approaches often stop at an averaged view of customers' behavior. That's a shame, because even if an average reveals a bottleneck in the process, the real insights for understanding and acting on that bottleneck come next, when we unpack those averages along logical dimensions and segments.

Take a look at the following graph comparing the recent Attract/Engage/ Convert Performance of leading online retailers. The size of each bubble in the diagram represents the number of unique visitors per month for each retailer. The horizontal axis shows how often each visitor comes to the retailer's site each month. The vertical axis shows each retailer's conversion rate—the rate at which visitors become buyers. (Of course, smart web analysts will distinguish between visitor-based and visit-based conversions statistics. In so doing, they will also note that there are probably some apples to oranges comparisons in these numbers.)

Figure 10: Ecommerce Operating Benchmarks

There's a bubble of medium size roughly in the middle of the chart that represents a firm with average performance. Looking around at some of the surrounding firms can help you put this performance into context and uncover potential opportunities for improvement.

If we wanted to find those opportunities, we would first have to filter out non-comparables. For example, it might be helpful to distinguish pure online players from multi-channel/store-intensive retailers whose customers might research online and buy in the store.

Next, we might look north, south, east, and west inside the diagram to identify firms whose performance suggests some apparent advantage or deficiency, and see if we can explain that difference by exploring the experience they're providing. Does a big ad campaign have weak connections to online channels? Where traffic is strong but repeat visits are not, how subscribe-able is the firm's experience? Are good shopping experiences compromised by checkout procedures with too many required clicks?

Add a time dimension. See if news about competitors moves them in a direction you might predict. Do this with other variables you systematically track as well, including social media statistics or search engine page rank on key product categories.

You can generalize this analysis and use it to look at customer segments. Simply substitute customer segments for competitors. For example, you can define customers by size, by geographic region, by the content you've exposed them to, including different products, pricing and associated discounts.

Direct marketers are already very familiar with this type of segmentation. They frequently manage catalog mailings according to customer deciles based on recency-of-order, frequency-of-order, average-order-size or other models. Different offers, or different mailing frequencies, go to each decile. If you engage your customers online, you can push this even further, until you are dynamically personalizing offers to individual customers as their responses suggest makes sense.

Practical Limits

There are limits to the utility of de-averaging performance. For example, unless you engineer processes that add marginal variety at virtually zero cost, that marginal variety can become very unprofitable.

Even if you can't or don't want to vary execution at a very granular level, de-averaging can still be very useful by helping you to uncover unseen influences on your marketing results. I worked with one client who was struggling to explain variances in the conversion responses of customers in different cities to a national media campaign. By studying these variances we identified an important new variable we would otherwise have been blind to. We observed that marketing efforts in another division, targeted at different customers but with some overlap with those targeted in our business, appeared to materially skew the results we attributed to our media investments. As a result, we found ways to coordinate marketing efforts across business units for their mutual benefit.

De-Average to Predict

So far, though we may be better informed by de-averaging performance, we're still managing through the rear-view mirror. The big promise of Big Data is of course to build models that use past performance to predict future outcomes. Yet, the potential accuracy of a prediction will be limited by the data's sample size and the variance within that sample. De-averaging performance may help you look forward with more confidence, whether you do it longitudinally by splitting the past into finer slices of time, or cross-sectionally, by splitting customers into finer segments.

If the data exists, why has it been so hard to leverage? Most marketing executives get exposed to predictive models in one of two ways. They may receive mix models built by agencies or other advisors to answer questions such as, "How relatively effective were print and search?" They may also receive answers from multi-channel optimization services that have been automatically generated by complex algorithms. While both are useful, each type of model has important disadvantages that marketers should recognize and deal with. In reports from advisors, the output is often presented as a professional brief created by statisticians for statisticians. As such the data is often static and thus quickly obsolete. In the latter case, the output is dynamic, but sits inside a black box. Executives may struggle to see whether an 80-20 version would provide a superior ROI. We've sought to move our clients into a middle zone where we help to operationalize—update and apply—more transparent and relatively lean models.

Update and Apply

Building a mix model these days is an expensive proposition. However, most of the work goes into getting, understanding, and adjusting the data. Many times, the data is not stored or staged in a way that others can use. This is true whether the work is done by agencies, consulting firms, or internally. Having gone through all of the trouble to activate and document sources, it's a shame to see the effort stop with just the first version of a model. If you stop at this point, then in subsequent efforts you will have to rediscover, re-prime, and re-learn all of the plumbing a year or

25

more later. And yet, the jump from one-time to recurring modeling isn't as expensive as you might think. The process of making modeling efforts even partially dynamic gets you used to thinking in terms of models, so you stay fresh with it.

Revving models more frequently also drives you to think in terms of automating the analysis process. You do this by generating scenarios that pose and answer the question, "What if?" For example: "If [dependent variable] looks like it's going to come in at A level, let's execute X action. If [dependent variable] looks like it's going to come in at B level, let's execute Y action." This makes for a much more transparent, deliberate, and forward-looking decision process. In short, if this modeling is worth doing once every year, it's probably worth doing four times a year, because the marginal cost really drops once you automate data gathering and analysis, even partially.

What's so lean about this multiple modeling method? Here's the complicated answer. You use multivariate regression techniques to predict the degree to which any conclusion about an independent variable's effect on a dependent variable is statistically probable. This is good, since you'd like to rule out variables that aren't reliable, and avoid paying for them in the future. You can also spare appropriate audiences the horror of talking about variables that don't make the cut. When you build a predictive model using the results of the multivariate regression, using a process called Stepwise Deletion, you end up tossing out the statistically questionable independent variables, anyway.

But the flip side of this is that sometimes the folks who build these models will seek sample sizes that allow them to set these probability thresholds quite high. Two things happen as a result. First, sampling costs, if applicable, go up. Second, you lose sight of variables you might otherwise consider in your model under different conditions. You can also lose sight of other dependent variables you might want to model.

This matters because most regressions assume that, if samples are involved, actual results are normally distributed around sample results. In practice, this might not be true. So, again, what does it mean to have a *lean* multiple modeling method? It means that, over time, you trade off the number of variables you include in your model to optimize for simplicity, with the cost of the incremental variables you include on your model's farm league payroll. In conjunction, you find creative ways to boost your sample.

As a general rule, I expect to see ~2 to 4 meaningful variables worth considering (explanatory power + probability), plus 2 to 4 candidates worth keeping an eye on. This heuristic shapes how we try to operationalize models that we can crank 2 to 4 times per year.

FOUR

Pragmalytic Techniques and Heuristics

By now, you have a skeleton for framing your mix optimization decisions. You have some ideas for connecting experiences, and sifting performance information that will help you make those decisions better. This chapter presents a set of techniques that can further improve your decisions and make the analytic process more efficient as well. They include:

- Frame your analysis in from needs, not out from capabilities
- Do the business math first
- Prioritize analysis on feasible solutions
- More importance + More uncertainty = More analysis (and *vice versa*)
- Know when to model, ask, or test
- Frame it as a story

Frame Your Analysis In From Needs, Not Out From Capabilities

A couple of years ago Force Five Partners pitched our marketing analytics agency service to a CEO in the retail industry. "That's nice," he said. "But my real issue is that I'm behind plan in my direct-to-consumer segment. Can you help me with that?" (Fortunately, we did.) From then on, we knew that all discussions about enabling capabilities had to be framed in the context of solving specific business challenges we'd identified. It was an important reminder for us as we built our business.

Clients often ask which analytics package, which modeling tool, or which tagging solution they should buy. There are two ways to reply. The wrong way is to answer with the name of a product or tool or solution. The right way is to pick up the thread from the analytics framework in Chapter One:

- What customer behavior are you trying to better understand or enable?
- How specific do you need your answers or capabilities to be to make a decision?
- How much would it be worth it to make a change? What are the stakes associated with a decision? (See the section on Business Math below)
- How much money and time have you got?
- Is addressing this question with this money and time a priority compared to your other needs?

Only when you have answers to these questions should you begin to evaluate a tool, a campaign or a solution.

Do the Business Math First

Some of the organizations we've worked with spend billions of dollars on marketing overall. Yet, some of their specific, targeted marketing initiatives represent a much more limited potential value than you might think. If you forget this, it's so easy to blow the analytics budget associated with setting up a single campaign and evaluating it afterward, particularly in the context of a small—say, mid-six-figure to low-seven-figure—contribution margin opportunity. Whenever a client presents a business problem or asks for a proposal, we always run some quick numbers about the potential magnitude of the costs and benefits of tackling the issue. The times we have failed to do this, we have regretted it.

For example, let's say you have a campaign idea spanning email and your web site. Assume that you have a target segment that numbers 500,000 people. Let's further suggest that you might expect an average order size of $100, with a $40 gross attribution margin per order (net of shipping costs and promotions).

Assume the following performance across the funnel:

- 15 percent email open rate
- 15 percent click-through rate from each opened email
- 5 percent conversion rate on each click-through from email

Simple math tells you that of the 500,000 people who receive the campaign, 75,000 may open the email. Of those, 11,250 are likely to click through. Of those, 563 are likely to place an order, each contributing $40, which means the campaign may yield $22,500.

- That $22,500 must pay for the mailing itself, both creative and distribution costs. It also has to cover overhead and leave some room for profit.
- If you assume that you want to apply just 10 percent of that total toward figuring out the target segment as well as tagging everything properly to evaluate results, then you have a budget of $2,250 to work with.
- If you run this campaign once a week during the year, you've got a little over $100,000 to spend on analytics for this approach. This budget must cover tools, help, time, everything.

If you don't have actual numbers such as the number of visitors, the rate of engagement, the rate of conversion, the average order size, or the contribution margins available, you can work the problem backward. You can ask, "Given that this decision will cost $X to vet and implement, what improvement scenarios for those numbers would yield sufficient returns?"

You can also ask what risk-adjusted payoff you expect from a campaign or decision. For example, increasing each of the above metrics by 10 percent changes the numbers substantially. Now you have:

- An average order size of $110
- Open and click-through rates move to 16.5 percent each
- A conversion rate of 5.5 percent

This raises the value of each mailing from $22,500 to nearly $33,000. If you assume execution costs remain the same, and you mail once a week, those 10 percent gains would be worth an incremental $500,000 a year. In order to compensate for risk and timing or ramping effects, you might assume that you're looking for a 3 to 1 return. In that case, you would be willing to spend about $165,000 on developing and implementing good ideas for this project.

Remember that there is almost always a solution that costs 20 percent as much that delivers between 40 and 60 percent of the benefit. This solution is usually simpler and less time-consuming to implement and maintain. For example, a retail client needed to increase conversions from a gift-suggestion program. With one configuration change to the algorithm for suggesting gifts to online shoppers, the client was able to double the number of additions to the online shopping basket. Experience says people respond mostly to burning platforms, with a bias to spend as little as possible until they absolutely have to. By and large, this bias is healthy. The universe of things that would make a big difference to customers is limited, and composed largely of small, clever add-ons rather than big complicated capabilities.

When I say this, people sometimes protest. "Typical business guy," they say. "Crushing hard-to-measure ideas prematurely with the ROI hammer!" Not at all. When it's your money, it's your call. But whether the stakes are high or low, let's experiment cheaply and feasibly first, and move to more exotic solutions when we can act on experience rather than intuition.[7]

---

[7] http://blogs.hbr.org/hbr/mcafee/2010/01/the-future-of-decision-making.html

Prioritize Analysis on Feasible Solutions

The analytics world is abuzz with talk about *emergent segmentation*. Basically this means that we stop hypothesizing what segments might make sense based on differential response or conversion rates and profitability. We tell the Big Data machines to find collections of customer characteristics that correlate well with these metrics. This is fine, if you have the money and time for it. Most people don't. Even if you do have the resources for this kind of search, the segments you discover are often expensive to target if the promising characteristics come in an external data vendor's file.

Don't misunderstand. Rolling around in the data, both directly and through automated agents, has its place. At Monitor Group's Marketspace unit, we researched differences between one service firm's business and persona-use customers, particularly how they each used marketing channels to research and buy. The startling finding about this ex-ante segmentation? There was no difference! Rather, when we looked at the hundreds of unique ways our respondent sample used the channel system for ordering services, we found a majority used fewer than ten unique routes. We used those preferred routes to re-define our segmentation scheme.

One segment of customers preferred in-person interactions, such as booking a repeat service visit at the client's physical location. We called this segment "People people." Cool! But how do you recognize such people so you can target them at the top of the funnel? It turns out "People people" skew significantly on certain demographic and other markers. Right, but skew = probability, not certainty. That meant we needed a targeting rule set that was weighted to reflect the probability of someone being a people person, once it had eliminated other deterministic targeting variables.

Of course, you can do this, too. But you may want to exhaust more feasible marketing opportunities for your hypothesized segments before you look for and figure out how to target emergent ones.

More Importance + More Uncertainty = More Analysis (and *vice versa*)

At Bain and Monitor, I was lucky to work with very intelligent and highly motivated people. One of the things that separated the best from the rest at these firms was that they could distinguish analytic rigor from analytic effort, and focus the latter where it mattered most. They put their own and their teams' work effort behind the toughest, most expensive decisions a company would face with the least optionality and reversibility and where the inbound data and outbound consequences were the least clear. This not only made for better answers, but it created a pragmatism that clients appreciated. It also allowed for an efficiency that made the consulting teams' lives more sustainable.

That's fine if you have abundant time in which to sift through the information and come to a decision about where to focus, but how do you operate when time is tight? The answer is define and then guess at adequate answers through iterative, expanding time cycles (minute, hour, week, month) rather than on executing the analysis itself. To do this, you'll need to approach the scope of your analysis in a series of iterations. I call it the Answer Slam. It works like this:

- Get your team together and present the decision to be made or list the options from which you must choose.
- Give relevant analysts and managers between five and ten minutes to recommend and support a decision, based on what they know.
- Ask team members to rate the intrinsic quality of the answer based both on logic and facts.
- Now ask them to rate the answer in light of the importance and uncertainty surrounding the decision. Given the rewards, risks, resources, and time available, would they move to act, dismiss, or study further?
- Repeat this process on the surviving "study further" issues, in ever-expanding cycles of time—an hour, a day, a week, etc.

This approach has several benefits. The obvious one is that only stuff worth studying gets the lion's share of your attention. A less obvious benefit is that by focusing analysts on fewer issues, you simplify what they have to look at.

Corollary: Multiple "5@95s" Trump a "2@99"

A couple of years ago I was invited to the Middle East to help pitch an audience measurement project. Because we would have to deploy expensive measurement equipment, managing sample size creatively became important. We segmented our audience carefully and varied the margin of error and confidence level we applied to drive the size of the sample. Some folks we targeted for individual in-person, in-depth surveying. Other folks we decided would be under-weighted in our sample. The marketing priority for this later sample would consist of mass outreach with minimal variance in campaign execution for a limited set of products. That understanding allowed us to live with a 5 percent margin of error and a 95 percent confidence level ("5@95"). We were left with a pool of folks for whom a finer-grained understanding was necessary for better targeting. By eliminating or relaxing the need for sampling in the other segments, we focused our sample size here to support a 2 percent margin of error and a 99 percent confidence level ("2@99"). Using the segmented approach, we were able to cut our total required sample size by a third, and the project's proposed cost by 20 percent.

As a general proposition, the more sure you are of a hypothesis, the less statistical accuracy you need to confirm it. The more estimates you have available to interpolate a guess, the less accurate any individual estimate has to be. Supporting a 5@95 requires sample sizes a fifth to a tenth of what 2@99 requires. If you can get two or three 5@95s together and your fixed survey costs are low, you can come out ahead of the game, both in cost and time.

Data scientists are difficult to find and expensive to hire. When you are ready to hire one, you want to make sure you can realize a return on this investment. Many times statisticians and vendors who shape research costs don't fully understand the contexts of the marketing decisions they support. It's important to ask questions about costs and sample sizes and to know how much statistical accuracy you need to confirm a hypothesis. Marketing executives who can focus sophisticated efforts only where complexity counts can make good decisions at a much lower cost and therefore realize a higher ROI.

When to Model, When to Ask, When to Test

There are three analytic approaches to deciding what to present to whom, and when: modeling, asking, and testing.

The Case for Modeling

You want to predict customer behavior, and in particular, customer response to help you decide on things you put in front of them. You have two choices. You can use your own data to build a predictive model, or you can buy a model developed by someone else that describes how folks similar to your customers respond to messages similar to those offered by your company.

There are some wonderfully sophisticated customer response models out there, developed by some really intelligent people, both inside companies for their own use and by vendors for sale to others. You may eventually end up with one of those. On the other hand, similar models, and blind faith in them, helped produce the current economic crisis. So how do you decide how much emphasis to put on modeling?

First, consider the quality of the data you have rather than the quantity. It doesn't matter how much data you have if it isn't good. How can you judge the quality of the data? One way is to ask where it comes from, and what happens to it on its way to you. If there are lots of manual and complex things that have to happen to it along the way, such as manual collection or fragile automated collection, if there are rollups or transformations across taxonomies in flux, your Spidey-senses should tingle. The second way to judge data quality is to ask a simple question against it, and see if the answer makes sense.

For example, at Force Five Partners we recently spotted an opportunity to personalize an online retailer's deal feed. We plugged an RSS feed of all the retailer's deals into a simple new service that allowed its users to choose what kinds of deals they were interested in. The service then provided a daily email summarizing deals of interest to those customers. We promoted the new service through email to the firm's customers, and found that visitors to the landing page were signing up at nearly a 40 percent rate. But then we searched the data to find out how many of the click-throughs on the deals presented were converting. In this case we chose a sample size of 7,000 and found that the answer was zero. According to the data, none of the click-throughs were converting. Given that deals presented through a feed that was not personalized had a higher conversion rate, we suspected a gremlin in the data.

Even if you have great data, you still need to evaluate the overall predictive ability of the model. Why? Because there are two ways to build a model. One is to boil the ocean, go completely overboard, test all the variables in every combination and see what works. Even if you have the computing power to do that, you will still spend a lot of money and end up with a lot of information to unpack and act upon.

The other way is to start with an idea about which variables might work and build from there. At Force Five Partners, by looking carefully at the relationships among the data we have before we start modeling, we have found that it is generally possible to identify between two and four variables that drive 60 percent of the predictive ability of a model. To go beyond that, you often need to consider many more variables. Because each additional variable adds more cost, complexity, and confusion, and because each additional variable adds value at a diminishing rate, it's prudent to see what decisions you can support using just those three variables, and which ones require more information to work through.

Here's an example. Quantcast.com is a service that allows you to profile the demographics of visitors to your web site. Publishers using the Quantcast service stick a Quantcast tracking pixel on their web pages and this allows Quantcast to track visitors to those sites using cookies. Now Quantcast can track those folks across all sites in the Quantcast network.

Some Quantcast publishers tag particular things on their sites as being associated with certain demographic characteristics. As visitors touch these tagged items, they are actually collectively describing themselves demographically. For example, users who click on products or messages in Bliss' anti-aging section can be presumed to be older women with money. By profiling the visitors' behaviors across many sites, Quantcast can profile the visitors. In this way I, as a Quantcast publisher, can infer my visitors' demographics, such as age income, race, gender, along with much more nuanced patterns of behavior than I could ever get from web analytics tools. All of these inferences would be based on the other sites my visitors frequent.

The variable that sits at the core of this model is browsing habits. Admittedly, browsing habits are themselves difficult to categorize. How many sites does a user have to visit, executing how many different actions before we can assume an appropriate level of accuracy demographic inferences? These aren't the only limitations to this basic model. Some limitations involve the interruption of data collection. For example users may exhibit different browsing habits on work computers than they do at home computers. Some users may delete cookies regularly. These are of course important for Quantcast to address in order to have a commercially viable product people can trust. But this company is planning to sell the service over and over again, to support a wide variety of decisions by marketers, advertisers, and publishers. You, on the other hand, may have more limited, focused needs.

Does a model based on browsing habits work when it is carried out in a much more limited scope? Our clients have used this approach to segment visitors to their own website based on which product pages visitors look at. Once they can define groups of visitors based on different behavior patterns on the site, they can unpack the conversion performance of individual pages visited by these different segments. De-averaging customer behavior into segments shows us where the conversion rates are best, and where they are weakest for each segment. In some cases, I have seen double-digit differences in conversion rates. Armed with this information, you can review differences in design that may account for this disparity. You can use these to review site design guidelines and then test and roll out best practices as broadly as you like. And you don't have to stop there. You can slice these segments geographically, and ask the model whether visits, revenues and profits are concentrated in certain geographic areas. Many of our clients find that geography is an important variable, and begin to test geo-tailored content. In these cases, using a model-based approach in which customer-browsing behavior as the central variable can yield enormous opportunities to create value.

The Case for Asking

Primary research is in decline for several reasons. Surveys and focus groups are notoriously prone to sample bias. Also, there is an enormous rift between what people say that they do and what they actually do. Yet when primary research is properly focused, it can be very helpful to understanding the reasons behind customer behavior.

Not that creating surveys is easy. No one likes to take a marketing survey, even a very short one. In my experience a short survey contains no more than a couple of profiling questions followed by a couple of substantive questions. Never ask the respondent anything that you should already know. Bribes don't work, either. If the sum of money is small, people won't bother. If the sum offered is too generous, people will say anything just to get to the payoff. (Donations to charity on behalf of the respondent, at least in my experience, have been an exception to this.)

One way to get around the problem of short attention spans is to ask just one question. After collecting a certain number of discrete answers, you can then present a graph or a snapshot of how the respondents' answers compare. I tried this by asking respondents to report how many free articles they would like to get from the *New York Times*, and how much they would be willing to pay to view each article afterward. (The results are here: http://www.octavianworld.org/octavianworld/2010/01/whats-nytcom-worth-to-you.html)

If you can administer a survey face-to-face, you can rely a little on social pressure to get people to be gracious once they agree to talk to you. Many won't agree to do that because they are in a hurry. The best primary research is conducted where you can observe people doing the thing that you want to learn more about, such as choosing a product from a crowded shelf. Ideally, you are observing them in their own environment rather than in an artificial product testing facility.

The bottom line is that using primary research to *identify* patterns in customer behavior is generally a poor investment. Instead you should use primary research to *understand* a pattern. And always respect the respondent's time. Don't field any survey you wouldn't tolerate on a busy day.

The Case for Testing

Testing is all the rage. It has never been easier or more affordable to try different marketing executions for the same product, or to run simultaneous promotions with tiny differences in anything from ad design elements to pricing. Many of the available tools for testing are powerful and easy to use. Some of them are free. But testing has two important limitations, each of which can be overcome. To do so, you'll need to organize yourself in ways that require some planning and investment.

First, you'll need to remember that each execution needs to be developed, whether it's a price, a bit of text, a graphic, a larger call to action button, a video or some combination of these. This can get expensive. The best way to organize these elements is to create modules of elements. In this way, elements can be assembled on the fly and isolated for the purposes of analytics. To do this, you need to tag your elements, and store them so that they can be added to campaigns easily in real time. In this way you can document past usage as well as the results for each element.

Second, you need to remember that testing means tracking results, and tracking the results of dozens or hundreds of simultaneously moving parts can make your head hurt. One way to manage the pain is to distinguish between the two types of testing you should be doing. You need to distinguish between the big decisions you test less frequently and the smaller decisions that you need to tweak all the time. Let's think of these big, less frequent decisions as "macro-optimization," and we can refer to the smaller, continual tests as "micro-optimization." While looking at each type of optimization, as a practical matter you can ignore variations in the other.

One financial services firm we worked with several years ago had lots of different things to put on its home page, such as ads, partner promotions, and teasers for services. In addition, there were all the navigation elements and other information. Here's how you might organize a test plan, broadly, for this situation:

- Macro-optimization tests the prominence of each type of information on the website. At holiday time, the organization might be tempted to give partner promotions a more prominent place on the page, which requires an alternative page structure. How often should alternative page structure appear? When and to whom should it appear? The test allows you to look the yields day-by-day for each page as a whole, and throttle each page structure's share of rotations accordingly, ignoring what's inside each content area.

- Micro-optimization tests different options inside each element on the home page. Here the organization can test the relative probable value per impression of each offer. It sets a starting rotation schedule to determine how often to present each offer and when and to whom. The only objective of the test is to determine the relative performance of each offer in each section across time. The organization can ignore where on the page the offer appeared. As offers out-perform their predicted value, they'll get more rotations, and as they lag, they'll have fewer rotations.

The Mix of Modeling, Asking, and Testing

As you can see from this last example, modeling and testing can often be combined. Your model will inform a starting rotation schedule for a variation to be tested. Then you update your model with the results of your tests, and whatever surveys or other primary research you do. A good analytic program relies on all three, and uses each appropriately.

Ideally, you automate these connections. As folks act on the tests you offer them, these results update your model dynamically. The model drives your rotation scheduling mechanism, although it should do this non-exclusively and with room for manual override. Your rotation scheduling mechanism is implemented in your content management system, your testing tool, your commerce platform, or through a separate bit of custom code. Eventually, you might dynamically connect the results of quantified surveys you conduct, once you've got them fine-tuned.

Frame It As a Story

Our local technology trade association, MITX.org, put on a panel discussion a few years ago, called "Measurement 2.0." The panelists stressed the importance of using stories as organizing mechanisms for analysis.

One of the panelists was Matt Cutler, who was at the time the CMO of Visible Measures, a video measurement vendor. Cutler talked about the importance of stressing to advertisers the importance of framing business problems and solutions as stories. "As humans, we're tuned to listen to stories deep in our DNA, and it's much harder to infer them from oceans of data and analyses." His remark suggests to me that there's an opportunity for a service that collects stories as hypotheses, so that you can test the fit between stories and stats, in the style of Mad-Libs.

Charlie Ballard, the COO of One to One, an interactive agency, told a story about how his company had tracked the story of a single user through his cookie ID. This user—nicknamed Anonymous User 110135—became the hero of a story told in a presentation to a cable company CEO. It was a huge hit. Ad agency VP, Mike Schneider of Allen & Gerritsen put it succinctly: "No story, no value."

This storytelling framework is a necessary component of analysis. Of course, any presentation relying on analytics should start with a presenter making a recommendation and briefly naming the analysis on which it's based. And yet it's crucial for the analyst to be able to cut through the data, the variables, the models and tests, the budgetary requirements and quickly move to a story about the customer's journey toward, through and beyond a purchase of a product or service. The customer story frames everything, and a successful presentation should end with an explanation of how the story changes because of the recommended action and how the company's bottom line will benefit.

At this point, you've read about and thought about a method to address the multi-channel marketing analytic challenge. While this method surely is not perfect, it does outline techniques to source and act on available information. The next questions are whether your infrastructure and your personnel are ready to use these techniques. In the next two sections, I'll discuss the technical and human dimensions involved.

PART II

The Technical Dimension

FIVE

Data Integration for Better Experiences and Targeting

Now you have a framework for organizing your approach to marketing analytics. Using that framework, you can re-integrate your perspective on how customers interact with you. You can de-average your understanding of these interactions. You also have suggestions for specific analytic and communications techniques you might apply.

Of course, these suggestions are all theoretical. In order to do any or all of these things, you will need to connect data that has been generated across channels and across the consumer experience.

This chapter looks at:

- How to string together data from different channels in order to personalize an experience, make an experience more seamless.
- How connecting data further illuminates your understanding of customer habits, and allows you to anticipate and respond to their future needs.
- The general forms of data that different channels can generate and use.
- Some ideas for logical two-channel connections that can help you bridge to the multi-channel future.

A number of research sources suggest that giving the customer a personalized experience can double the conversion rate in a buying process. As a corollary, you can expect a social referral to have the same impact, and the effects reinforce each other. So while realizing this opportunity can become complicated, it's well worth exploring how much these opportunities make sense for you. The more your product or service offers a tremendous variety of options for customers, or if it is a complex product or service, or if the buying process itself is complex, the more likely you are to see returns from connecting and personalizing the customer experience to make it as relevant as possible for each customer.

Connecting Through Multiple Channels

In the second decade of the 21st century, the ability to connect and personalize experiences has gone pretty mainstream. For example, my family recently went to the Ninety Nine Restaurant (which is part of a regional chain) in Centerville, Massachusetts, on Cape Cod. Lying on the table was a pad of these forms:

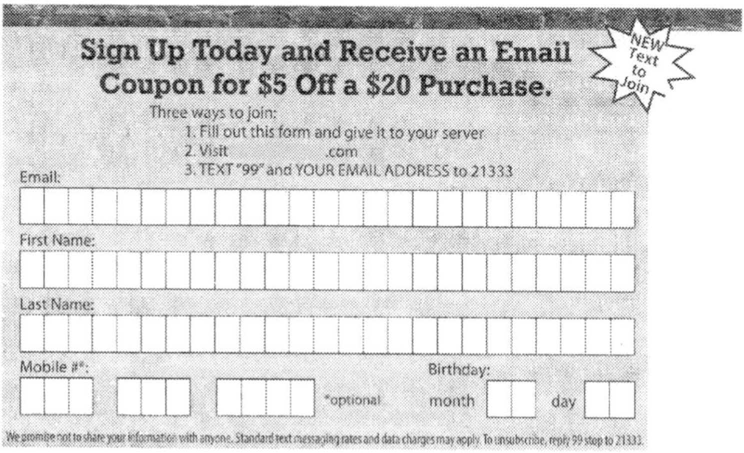
Sign Up Today and Receive an Email Coupon for $5 Off a $20 Purchase.

NEW Text to Join

Three ways to join:
1. Fill out this form and give it to your server
2. Visit .com
3. TEXT "99" and YOUR EMAIL ADDRESS to 21333

Email:

First Name:

Last Name:

Mobile #*: *optional

Birthday: month day

We promise not to share your information with anyone. Standard text messaging rates and data charges may apply. To unsubscribe, reply 99 stop to 21333.

Figure 11: Ninety Nine Restaurant Loyalty Form

I filled out the form, texted the numerals 99 and my email address to the number given, and twenty-four hours later this appeared in my inbox:

Figure 12: Ninety Nine Restaurant Landing Page

I clicked through to see this coupon:

Figure 13: Ninety Nine Restaurant Coupon

Restaurant to text to email to web and back to restaurant, all nicely connected. Cool! Unfortunately the coupon expired since I started writing this book. Looks like we'll have to sacrifice another family member's phone number. Wait a second. Maybe I'll use two phones to get two coupons and then ask for separate checks. (Times are tough!) This entire program has been run for Ninety Nine Restaurant by an external service, called Fishbowl Marketing. It's a good example of mainstream multi-channel marketing. But we could go even further!

Here are a few possibilities:

- Although texting the number 99 is clever, it's hardly informative. I could have been asked to text "Cape Cod" or "Cville" so that my sign-up could have been tracked by its location. This would allow the restaurant to compare sign-ups against store traffic across different regions. I am mindful that Fishbowl might need an SMS address unique to the Ninety Nine Restaurant client for this, and that's more expensive.
- I don't live on Cape Cod and may not return there anytime soon. Still, there are several Ninety Nine Restaurant locations near my home. The program could have directed me to these restaurants when I clicked through from the email to the landing page from my home computer. The server could have recognized the location of the request and returned a link to a map of nearby locations under the coupon—although most folks probably won't explicitly update their preferences, in part because of the unremarkable landing page copy exhorting them to do so. (And yet, here's a good testing opportunity!) This isn't the first time I've participated in this kind of offer. My cell phone number is out there and attached to other consumer preferences of mine. Fishbowl missed an opportunity to cross my cell phone number against other databases that also have it. By doing so they might have found other information that might help them personalize this offer to me.
- For example, the Ninety Nine Restaurant chain is owned by O'Charley's Inc., which also owns a chain of steakhouses called Stoney River. Maybe I've eaten at one of these other restaurants. If the program is set up at the corporate level, they could cross check their database for this information. If not, the company might suggest that I try these other restaurants anyway.
- Some sample of users could be asked to participate in a short exit survey about their experience in the restaurant, perhaps for additional benefits.

- Remember that social referrals are highly successful. So, where in this campaign do I have the chance to share the coupon with my friends and get an additional discount when they sign up to the e-club? I did get follow up email messages on holidays inviting me back to the restaurant. These messages did suggest that I invite friends along. Unfortunately, when I clicked through to the landing page to invite these friends, the forms asked me to identify myself, even though I hadn't cleared cookies from my browser in the interim.

- I'm also curious about the missing links to other social media sites, such as Facebook (where the chain seems to have a well-developed presence) and Twitter (where its presence is very limited). If I had links to these during my journey to the coupon, I might have gone to those sites to offer feedback or to look for other promotions.

- Finally, Fishbowl might consider using a mobile location-based service provider in order to offer loyalty rewards according to the number of check-ins at the restaurant. This could be part of the vendor branded experience or it could be part of a white label application developed off of vendors' APIs.[8] Capturing check-ins could allow the restaurant to take advantage of the viral marketing advantages of these services. For example, my friends would be notified whenever I check-in at the Ninety Nine. Of course, this begs the question of whether Ninety Nine Restaurant customers are leading-edge tech adopters with the latest smart phones and the associated Obsessive Check-in Disorder (OCD).[9] Maybe not yet, but what were we saying about Facebook a few years ago?

Which of these ideas should Fishbowl pursue, if any? As we've seen so far, the answer depends on which customers they want to target. Also, where in the buying process can they find the greatest leverage for improving the customer experience and therefore the associated returns? This program is designed to drive loyalty, or at least to buy return visits. It solely targets people already sitting inside one of their restaurants. And that leads to another question: Is there any good reason why the invitation to text an

---

[8] http://thenextweb.com/location/2010/03/16/foursquare-dennis-crowley-talks-revenue-api-brands-badge/

[9] http://www.youtube.com/watch?v=Gpypn-JIPng

email address to get a coupon didn't run in a television or radio spot, in a print ad, on a billboard, or as part of an event sponsorship? If it had, the company could have harnessed the ability to link upstream awareness to engagement and then conversion. Does the greatest opportunity for this restaurant chain lie in attracting and converting new customers or does it lie in generating multiple return visits from current customers? The answer to that question should drive all subsequent questions about how to best fashion this campaign. This is why it is so important for companies to look past the data that each channel can pump out individually. Instead they should focus on ways to use the data generated by each channel to track customers. They need to understand the role of each channel and its weight in moving customers along. Only then can companies invest pragmatically in channels that will produce the greatest return.

Designing for Trackability

A touchpoint can be defined as any moment when a person engages with a company or one of its messages. A customer experiences a touchpoint while shopping in a store, visiting a company website, calling a call center, even looking at a magazine ad or a billboard. Each one of these touchpoints could generate lots of information that can help the company focus and shape the person's experience.

Nonetheless, few companies design company interfaces with the idea that customer engagement can and should be tracked. For example, let's say you put up a billboard and include a deep link (www.yourco/unique-landing-page.html). Here's what information you can get about every person who visits that page:

- Identification of the source channel. You can do this by media type, or by individual ad. If you want to do the latter, you can code the URL for a landing page that is unique to an individual billboard.
- All the information the browser brings with it. Collectively, this can get pretty close to fingerprinting the user uniquely[10] even

---

[10]   https://panopticlick.eff.org/

without the help of extra tracking functions, such as cookies, crucial in an age where privacy concerns increasingly make third party cookies obsolete for tracking.

- Location of the intermediary server, the name of the organization running the server and its communications node. This is less useful if a user surfs from a proxy server run by, say, Comcast. Still, it can be very useful if you are selling BMWs to Goldman Sachs bankers.
- All the cookies stored and information on other data storage constructs such as Adobe's Flash Local Shared Objects[11] that have been sent to the browser by the server. This can include messages and information sent during the current browsing session.

The information from cookies and data storage constructs is worth emphasizing because you can harvest so much information from this alone, including:

- The identity of the user, if the user has provided this in the past and if the cookie that stored it has not been deleted or has been updated during the browsing session.
- Details of past and current browsing activity, including the pages visited, the actions undertaken, information submitted on your web forms or programs, or other digital properties.
- Tracking tags, special URLs and other variables that you have customized to add further meaning to the raw data coming back. For example, you might tag a page as belonging to a particular product group or as having been accessed from a link associated with a particular seasonal campaign.

While all this information creates enormous opportunity, it also creates enormous responsibility to lead and follow on the privacy front. Several organizations are sending up warning bells to consumers about how their privacy is in jeopardy. The Electronic Frontier Foundation has also written a series of articles[12] for users on how they are being tracked, often by companies acting in willful violation of their own privacy policies and laws.

---

[11]   http://en.wikipedia.org/wiki/Local_Shared_Object

[12]   https://www.eff.org/deeplinks/2009/09/new-cookie

One study shows how readily browsers can generate a unique fingerprint and how easily this fingerprint can be exploited. (https://panopticlick.eff. org/) Just as Wall Street has evolved compliance functions, we are likely to see these emerge in digital marketing after a few more scandals. (One might add, cynically, that we should expect them to be about as effective.)

Now that SMS-capable devices have become ubiquitous, and smartphones nearly so, deep links are so five years ago. Why put a deep link on a billboard with the hope that a passerby writes down the link and visits it later from a quaint PC? Now advertisers had better be aware of 2D barcodes, SMS addresses, QR codes, and location-based services (LBS) apps, and the list is growing. Before long, Augmented Reality[13] will further enrich and compress the timelines of customers' experiences, by wrapping additional digital context around the physical world in real time.

The ability to immediately interact with upstream media will of course have an interesting effect on the assumed value of awareness investments in them. If no one can interact with a billboard, how is it possible to know whether its presence has value in creating impressions? Once you can measure the traffic around the billboard, and once you can measure the rich interactions that people have with it via personal devices, then you know much more about its value. And what if people ignore it? Shops and clubs still hire folks to pass out flyers to remind and encourage would-be patrons to stop in. In the future, these flyers will be offered as digital bookmarks. People will have the ability to opt-in to receive these offers either for immediate or deferred response. And they will be able to opt-in or out according to firm, category, location, or through social networking friends. While this allows companies to collect information on engagement, it also allows them to collect information on rejections, on the number of potential customers who opt-out, in effect saying, "Sorry, not interested." When that happens, what should companies infer about the value of that brand impression?

---

[13]   http://en.wikipedia.org/wiki/Augmented_reality

Information Integration for Enhanced Targeting

So, on one level you want to design each touchpoint so that you can gather the information about customer behaviors and interests. The next step is to see how you might link this information to the other sources you have available. By linking even a single element of information to other sources, you can further personalize and optimize the customer experience.

Let's say for example that a user's browser requests a page from your server. The browser sends you the header of the request and along with it comes the last cookie your server sent there. This cookie lets you know that you can associate this request with jimmyb007@gmail.com (assuming he has given you this information, presumably in a subscription). Any other data set associated with this email address is a potential aid to deciding how to treat Mr. Bond. These data sets may be those that you have generated or purchased or subscribed to, and they may include your CRM system, any credit data you have, or any lifestyle or psychographic segmentation service you use. If you participate in an ad network, either as an advertiser or a publisher, some of this information may also be used (subject to privacy controls) to better target ads that appear on your site or on other websites. Other identifying information can also make its way to your analytics vendor once its tag does its job of gathering and relaying information it collects. Some analytics vendors now offer the ability to divine and apply emergent, high-converting customer segment definitions automatically.[14]

Let's assume you run an auto rental agency in Montenegro that caters to wealthy gamblers. It might make sense to stage some of the additional data you have in your CRM system for a real-time lookup when Mr. Bond surfs into your site, perhaps even before he logs in. Does he have a history of treating your fine cars aggressively? Perhaps you should feature the Hummers on your lot first.

---

[14]   http://www.mediapost.com/publications/?fa=Articles. showArticle&art_aid=125430&nid=112904

Alternatively, let's say your agency's account executives suggest you advertise online through a behavioral targeting ad network, in which the Casino Royale is a member. In this case, the hotel's guests see your ad on the hotel's web page when they log in from their rooms. A real-time check of other sites Mr. Bond has been browsing might help in deciding whether to show him the Aston Martin DBS or a Renault Logan. Bond might be flush from a baccarat-beat-down of the villain Le Chiffre, in which case he may have been surfing NetJets.com for flights to Capri. If his fellow agent Vesper Lynd has just denied his request for additional funds from Her Majesty's Treasury, Bond might be browsing EasyJet.com for flights home, or perhaps Airtiming his CIA counterpart Felix Leiter on Facebook to hitch a ride. Of course, this fictional scenario simplifies how you might target a named user. In practice, privacy regulations and processes govern this type of behavioral targeting. The actual process would match an anonymous visitor's clickstream against the behavior of other anonymous users to decide what content to show.

The decision to pursue these data augmentations would hang on the incremental value of doing so. You would need to consider the value to your bottom line as well as the value added to Mr. Bond's experience. In fact, you can often test the value of additional information such as this to discover which options offer the greatest value. But rather than passively pursuing test after test, or modeling variable after variable, or listening to pitches about different possible solutions, you should do some advanced thinking about the various information options at hand. Here's a sorting exercise that might be helpful:

1. Where is the need greatest? Evaluate this by segment, by buying stage or between different channels.

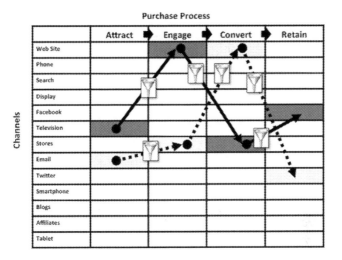

Figure 14: Buying Process Yields by Target Segment

2. What information is available to us to work with there? What other data can we link to this?

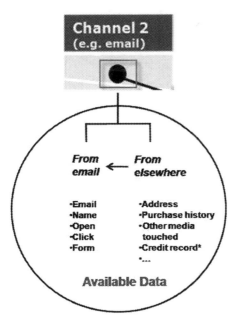

Figure 15: Available Data

3. Of the available options, which data is potentially valuable? Which information would shape what you present to a customer or change how you handle a customer or prospect in a way that's likely to significantly improve the odds of conversion, at least to the next step?

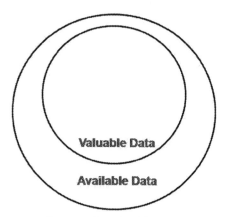

Figure 16: Valuable Data

4. Which option is practically actionable? Ask how you would get, process, and apply this information? Evaluate to what degree these answers sound feasible and affordable.

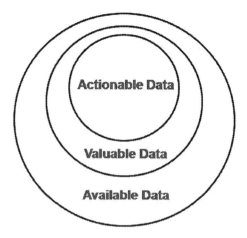

Figure 17: Actionable Data

Optimizing Two-Channel Connections

The best way to focus your interventions is to find the biggest breakdown between channels along the dominant pathway of a target customer segment. Here are some examples of these that in my experience provide good payoffs to your increased attention:

- Display ads and search results (organic and paid)—Display advertising has been shown to raise search activity. So, be sure the terms you use in your display ads are the ones you want folks to search for. These should be terms you rank well on organically or that are consistent with your paid search keywords.
- Click-to-Chat features that link web sites to live operators. Even the best-designed web sites can be challenging for some of the people you target. It's useful to provide this chat feature, particularly when the average order is a big ticket. On the other hand, you don't want to be deluged with requests. Offering an array of help resources, with self-help options visible before assisted help, can pay big dividends.
- Landing pages, and their precedents. One best practice is to think in terms of how much you ask of a user relative to what you offer that user. The trick is to optimize the distribution of what you ask for, and where, along the path. You might try thinking beyond the idea of landing pages and instead consider a multi-step landing experience.[15] This multi-step experience has the power to sustain the give-to-get balance all the way through to a conversion event.
- Events and social media. Events help give people something interesting or entertaining to share, photograph, tweet and post about. If you want high-quality output for your brand from social media, you need to inject your social media sites with lots of high-quality input. Events are the best source of this input because they are ultimately conversational. For example, you control the talent, meaning the speakers, the band, etc.
- Stores and ecommerce. The traditional view is that these channels are substitutes. Yet customers most often view them as synergistic.

---

[15] http://www.octavianworld.org/octavianworld/2010/02/beyond-ab-and-mvt-optimizing-experiences.html

They want to buy online and pick up in the store. They want to buy online while shopping in the store. And with the advent of "showrooming" shopping apps such as Red Laser, they may be shopping in one store while buying from a competitor. (Time to re-think your price matching policies.)

You may also ask: If one channel doesn't feed another, what's the opportunity for coordination? In this case, you might think about unifying and optimizing planning by including a broader set of channel substitutes. Remember to prioritize in terms of segment-appropriateness rather than brand consistency. Here are a few examples:

- Direct mail campaigns, including email and catalogs. Your direct mail plan will be executed typically across an RFM model (Recency, Frequency, Monetary Value), tracking customer X by the number of orders, how recently they were made and how much was spent on average in each order. Limiting the span of this model to direct, physical mail only could have you chop off cells containing customers of only marginal value if all you consider is their direct mail response; these might have paid off if you had swapped in emails for some of the drops in a campaign.
- Contextual display, TV, radio, print, outdoor, sponsorships. These awareness-stage investments target customers in what some call lean-back mode. This is different from the messages customers take in while surfing, texting, playing a game, or lean-forward mode. Your first instinct may be to keep brand messages consistent across a campaign, but a more important consideration is to make messages in each channel appropriate to the target segment that uses that channel most heavily in this awareness stage.
- Paid search and affiliate channels. Be sure to avoid paying double!

All this assumes, of course, that you have multiple channels in optimum working order. There is no point in connecting channels and personalizing them for this dynamic customer experience if you have a website that constantly crashes, or features an unusable design. If your call center pushes customers through a 12-step IVR and a 30-minute wait time for a live operator who can't help you or can't make himself understood, you have bigger things to worry about than underperforming connections—all the more reason why you have to be choosy with the ones you do connect, rather than painting your customer experience with the broad brush commonly seen today.

SIX

Pragmalytic Infrastructure: A Good Enough Approach to Data Management

At this point I've discussed techniques and caveats for optimizing your multi-channel mix, and executing multi-channel campaigns. But you can't do any of these things unless you have reasonably good data. When I say *good* data, I mean data that could be described as documented, clean, consistent, available, understood, connectable, and governed. There might be other descriptors for good data, but because I've never been to Data Nirvana, this is as far as my imagination goes.

So, you turn to IT to bring you good data. Next thing you know, they've launched a task force to create a data warehouse proposal. The information architects on this task force may run around talking about taxonomy and ontology and master data management. Six months later, you've got a spec, and a governance process to go with it, but no answers. Seven out of ten times, the whole effort collapses from its own weight.

Mostly, this isn't IT's fault. Information technology departments are often expected to support your decision-making, but rarely do marketing managers give them the opportunity to understand fully the strategic, operational, and financial contexts of the decisions being made. What they are likely to hear instead is a broad call to arms. And sometimes the decisions being made are changing faster than the provisioning process IT has created. When this happens, these guys feel themselves to be under constant pressure to provide better support without ever knowing how to predict what form that support is going to take. And so they end up confusing means for ends. They spend more time thinking about collecting and managing every piece of data just in case someone needs it. Instead, you want them focusing on gathering just what you ask for at the moment you need it.

Keeping Your Data House Clean Enough

As an alternative, you might consider laying out a much thinner layer of permanent data infrastructure. On this, you develop a planned series of spikes to handle decisions that carry high stakes, tight timing, frequent recurrence and that feature some form of complexity in sources (both the data itself and the organizations that provide it). Forrester Research marketing analyst Sean Corcoran memorably characterizes this continuum as CRAP: Collect-Report-Analyze-Predict. To this, I might add an E for Execute, which would describe situations in which predictions are wired into marketing platforms to fully automate the marketing processes. At Force Five Partners, we refer to this automation as "Fly-by-Wire Marketing."[16]

How clean is clean enough? Some folks are neat freaks and keep their houses in pristine condition. Others invite friends to dinner every now and then to motivate themselves to clean more thoroughly—at least that's how it seems to work in our house. Of course, cleaning up to entertain guests is a little easier if you have things under a sustainable level of control beforehand. The same holds true with collecting marketing data. You should think of this sustainable level of control as a data scaffolding, in order to contrast it with the more fully realized data warehouse efforts you may have attempted in the past.

---

[16]   http://www.octavianworld.org/octavianworld/2009/10/ flybywire-marketing.html

Five Steps to Data Scaffolding

1. Inventory your decisions.

The first step is simple. Ask yourself what decisions you are trying to support. What do you need to know to make these decisions? For example, you could ask what changes to customer targeting you need to make. What changes to channel mix do you need to make? What changes to campaigns should you make?

Where do you maintain your wish list for these decisions? This is a good job for an issue-tracker system, or ticket tracker, with the following format:

*   Decision
    Who is going to make it?
    When?
    How often?
    What's at stake? (detail the investment required, the returns at stake, or the risks involved)

*   Question
    Who needs to know?
    When?

*   Required data
    Who's going to analyze?
    When?

*   Required data attributes
    Organization of that data
    Accuracy
    Format
    Cost

2. Inventory the data you have and the data you need.

Next, you have to look at the data you already have and see what's missing. Where do you maintain your list of the data you've got? A simple Google spreadsheet would go a long way toward organizing this. Each row of the spreadsheet accounts for a separate data set, while the columns will include the data set's description, the keeper's name and contact information.

What if you execute campaigns through external service providers? This presents a complicating factor. These providers often fulfill campaigns using software-as-a-service infrastructures, which means that they maintain the data sets associated with those infrastructures outside the walls of the organization.

For example, consider the "Share This" button at the end of an article or a product listing. This is often a plug-in to your web site that comes from a third party, such as AddThis.com. Let's say you decide to pursue a viral marketing campaign and want to target readers or customers who regularly share your content with others using this feature. The plug-in provider lives outside your walls. It may or may not provide an administrative interface that allows you to see what got shared, and when it was shared (AddThis does offer this interface). If it doesn't, and if you fail to track the clicks on the share button in your primary web analytics tool, you will forgo visibility into who is sharing your content. Many analysts don't track these clicks because the organization is much more focused on how traffic comes in rather than how it goes out. The point is that when IT organizes analytics tools based solely on what it controls, you lose. Better to organize your efforts around what information the business needs in order to make relevant decisions. Remember to pitch a big tent.

You should also know how you store information in your customer database and for how long. Most organizations know to track customers based on what they have ordered in the past. Some databases might even inventory communications sent to each customer, such as catalogs, emails, as well as customer service interactions, including call center conversations. However, unless you are a major digitally-led firm, you are unlikely to have a fully-integrated customer clickstream database, one that tracks all customer interactions, including those on your web sites, on the other digital properties you sponsor, and on related third-party sites. At minimum you should know where this data lives, and ask about its lifespan. Some IT shops purge log files after a short while to save on storage costs. Make sure you know how to get at this information so that you don't lose it in a periodic purge. Better yet, figure out how you can stage it (see below) for ready access if the questions above suggest you might need it.

3. Assess the quality of your data.

Now, let's consider the quality of your data and its cleanliness. What processes does your organization use to generate data? Where in that process do things break down in a way that causes data captured to be incorrect or incomplete? What's the magnitude of the problem, in the context of decisions to be supported?

4. Understand your data.

How are data in various collections defined? Are these definitions sufficiently similar? In cases where you wish to reconcile or integrate data sets, do they share a common key such as a Social Security number or an email address? How are different sets of similar data rolled up? If you have different hierarchies for aggregating sets of data, you can have difficulties comparing them. For example, if you collect information on web traffic sources by location, you may find that some sources are tracked geographically, and then rolled up to city, state, or county levels. And yet other sources are tracked to a zip code that will be rolled up to a Metropolitan Statistical Area. These two data sets seem so similar and yet they will be difficult to correlate.

5. Determine data availability.

How do you get at the data you need? Where is it? Do you get it in batches, or is it available via a reliable feed or API? Is it available in a usable format? Who owns it, meaning who pays for it and who keeps it? To what degree is sharing restricted, through privacy policies or other non-disclosure restrictions?

Take a quick first pass at answering each of the questions as they relate to the quality and cleanliness of the data at hand. Look at your available data in terms of its consistency and connectivity. This is a perfect job for a wiki, ideally one that can be linked to the spreadsheet that keeps the master inventory of data.

Clean-Up as Means, Not Ends

Once, you might have been able to commission a project to take this quick first pass for its own sake. These days, any initiative not related to a near-term imperative is on the chopping block. So, you clean up as you go. The key, as described above, is to engage in a little lightweight documentation while you're at it.

Here's an example. A couple of years ago, Force Five Partners worked with a senior team that was sitting on a big proposal from IT. The proposal called for a data warehouse to help uncover opportunities for addressing media mix optimization. Not only were the team members concerned about whether to proceed with the plan, they also needed to decide on a channel mix for the coming year's budget and then submit it to the board.

We asked them how their customers liked to shop. We asked how the firm went to market. We identified an opportunity to increase the use of email in a direct mix dominated by traditional catalog mailings. When we asked why email wasn't a bigger part of the mix, the answer was that it had never earned its way into the mix.

Together, we looked at the numbers and found that the size of the house list for mailing catalogs was four times as large as the email list. That seemed odd. The company did not yet have a unified CRM system in place, so we mapped the flows of names from the database of each channel to the next. Here we found some broken plumbing. Names added to the house list weren't flowing into the email file. The reasons for this were technical and related to the failure of a system-to-system chron job.

Further, as we peeked into the email file itself, we found a bunch of names that were "pended," for reasons having to do with a previously solved whitelisting issue. By making a couple of quick fixes, we tripled the email list overnight.

With a substantial and growing email list in place and working better, the company could now consider email communication as a legitimate potential substitute for engaging marginally profitable catalog customers. Now, when the RFM model identifies unprofitable customers who should be dropped from a seasonal catalog campaign, those customers can instead receive seasonal emails that might trigger a purchase. Swapping email into the mix for marginally profitable customers reduces printing and mailing costs. In this case, the combination of higher contribution margin and savings in both printing and postage resulted in a greater than 40 percent improvement of the catalog channel—an eight-figure top line contributor.

Meanwhile, we set up a simple collaborative workspace on the web where we documented things as described above. We didn't think of this as extra work. We needed to track these variables ourselves in order to execute and communicate the improvements. By using this collaborative workspace, we could track these changes not only for the folks involved at the time, but also for future decision-makers.

In the end we had a twofer. We had moved the needle on the performance of the business, and in the process we had a much clearer, cleaner, better-documented idea of the data we were working with.

PART III

The Human Dimension

SEVEN

The Pragmalytic Marketer

Most organizations start by hiring analytic specialists and then tucking these new recruits into units meant serve as liaisons between marketing and IT. Only as an afterthought do these organizations consider educating line marketing managers on analytics, or developing a shared process and language for using these analytics.

I believe these priorities are backward.

My rule is this: *Don't hire analysts until you've evaluated and developed analytic marketers.*

If you put an analytic specialist into a group of specialists, that analyst's marginal time will go to developing more complex analyses. It's what they do. In many cases these new analyses will race ahead of your operating team's ability to use any insights these analyses produce.

What you want is to see insights and actions more tightly coupled. To get to this point, you need to follow Gandhi's advice and be the change you want to see in the world. The first step is to develop in your line product managers and channel managers a better understanding of analytics and its capabilities. You want these managers to become so fluent in the practical uses of analytics that this knowledge becomes embedded in their day-to-day decision-making. With this knowledge, they will make better decisions and choices about what kind of additional help they need. They will communicate more effectively with each other, with specialist analytic resources, with vendors and agencies, and with IT as well.

Where to start? Here's a diagnostic that can help you evaluate the members of your team in terms of their familiarity with analytics.

A Diagnostic for Analytic Decision-Making

Approach your team members, either individually or collectively. Ask them to produce a list of ideas for increasing revenues 10 percent over the next three years using existing resources. I use the three-year time frame so that team members have to consider increasing awareness as well as conversion. Give them a week and then observe their responses.

What are you looking for in these responses? At a basic level, you're just hoping for ideas. More important than the ideas, though, is how these ideas are framed.

- Each idea should be described against a backdrop of customer segments and the needs of customers in each segment.
- Several ideas are better than one, and yet you should pay particular attention to what inspired the idea. Is this an attempt to simply copy the direct competition, or has this person picked up his or her head and gone looking for sources in order to develop some informed perspective?

Next, look for the reasoning behind these ideas as they apply to you. Focus on the logic first and the data to support it second. Look at which data sources the team member used, check to see whether these sources were manipulated or coordinated to support the logical assumptions.

- Did the team member dig into the sources, integrate across them, and look beyond to new sources?
- How were data sources accessed and manipulated? Did the team member accomplish this alone, or with help from the manual, or with IT support? If there were data access issues, what caused them?

- Did the team member explicitly address data quality, and not lose the forest for the leaves on the trees?
- Was the data unleashed in a torrent or was it leavened with anecdotes and illustrative examples?

Once you've heard the ideas and whatever supporting data is available, you'll be looking to see some math that reconciles the ideas to the revenue target. Beyond that, you'll want to hear the team member's evaluation of the feasibility of the ideas. A team member who can do all of this is pretty impressive.

And yet, there's more. I would also be looking for a prioritization of the proposed ideas against each other. Finally, and this is the hard part, a team member should be able to state what the organization should do differently in order to make available the resources required to carry out the idea or ideas.

This list of expectations is helpful in several ways. It gives you a rubric to evaluate the sophistication of your team or of individual members in a way that's directly relevant to improving the performance of the business. Also, a team member's failure or a group's failure to give a specific answer at any level will alert you to the issues you need to be teaching. If team members can't answer specific questions or quantify the logic behind their ideas because of structural limitations or inconsistencies in the data available to them, you'll learn that, too. And you'll know that you need to work on ways to better support them.

Perhaps the best part of this exercise is that by running it regularly and keeping good track of the answers, you're building up great source material for the next time you need to submit a plan.

When You Hire Analysts

Let's assume you've encouraged your team to become great analytical marketers, and you've pushed them as far as you can. Now it's time to bring in some analysts at various levels to bridge the gap so that you can answer the questions posed by the Analytic Brief. What should you look for?

At the simplest level, I look for both substance and style. I break substance down into areas of knowledge I think a good analyst should have:

- What are the candidate's functional experiences with respect to different types of marketing—brand, inbound direct, outbound direct, social?
- What are the candidate's experiences and fluency with sector-specific knowledge?
- What are the candidate's technical experiences in terms of querying, modeling, testing, and researching?

Stylistically, I look for someone who doesn't live exclusively in a data bubble. In the introduction to this book, I described the people from Mars, incredibly intelligent and devoted to the intricacies of the data they can gather. You don't want just those qualities in an analyst. You want a nice mix of Venus and Earth, too: the ability to communicate and someone who understands execution and results.

I also like to see both breadth and depth of exposure. A great analyst has assembled a broad pattern library of experiences and models from which to draw. He or she should also have had the chance to drive a marketing initiative from insight generation through implementation, results, and learning in more than one situation. Breadth tends to be associated with experiences in agencies, consulting firms, or vendors, while depth tends to come from having a marketing role inside a firm.

But don't stop at tenure-based experience and skills. Look beyond the lines on the resume that state the number of years worked at which corporations and consulting firms, and the impressive list of software program fluency. Whether you're hiring a consultant or a full-time employee, a better way to hire is to screen for contributions to results and learning. People who think in terms of results and can tell a credible story about what their experiences have taught them are much more likely to integrate well with others. They are much more likely to get things done than they are to sit back as high priests who keep you in their thrall. Your interview questions might look like this:

- Describe an important business result that you helped achieve. What was the business, and what was the result?
- What was the insight behind this success? How did the business execute on it?
- Tell me about how you identified and developed this insight. In particular, what sources of data and information did you use? What did you do to divine a useful pattern out of them? How did you manage to keep your analysis efficient? What obstacles did you have to overcome, and how did you manage that?
- Tell me how you communicated this insight? How did you translate it from an idea into an action plan that people bought into?

Another filter to apply is the degree of analytic rigor a prospective consultant or job candidate has used to prepare for an interview. These days a business has many public faces, and there are a number of public data sources that describe the performance of its customer interfaces. These include Compete.com, Quantcast, Google Insights, Microsoft adLabs, Hubspot Website Grader, along with various social media sites, SEC filings, and trade magazines. Through these sources, an individual willing to do the research can develop a sense of your company's competitive position and perhaps form some suggestions or at least questions about the business. A good interview question to kick off this discussion might be, "Where in our business do you see room for improvement, and why?" Then listen not only for the suggestions themselves, but also for the logic and data that the candidate presents to support them.

Finally, I like folks who show rather than tell. Specifically, good analysts are active and visible online. They can take you through the Google Analytics profiles for their online properties. They play an active role in industry associations, and perhaps they have published in relevant places.

Be aware that few people will hit all these marks. So rather than viewing these strictly as screening criteria, you might also use them as the basis for a development plan for that diamond in the rough you hire!

EIGHT

The Pragmalytic Organization

Here's a concerning trend in marketing management today. Many firms have cut in-house staffing for marketing so drastically that they need to rely on partner relationships and vendor relationships to carry out more of their marketing initiatives. These firms may have relationships with display ad networks, search marketing firms, affiliate hubs, direct agencies that handle emailing or catalog mailings, and agencies that handle anything from public relations to social media. Some of these outside vendors and agencies operate as independent, black box providers. You give them money, have a couple of meetings to agree on the ground rules, and manage their output by some sort of metric—CPM, CPC, CPA. While you may call up the representative and ask some questions, stir the pot a little, in most cases each agency or vendor operates on its own. Inside the agency, the employees multiply, divide, regress, predict and execute on your behalf, but they do so blinkered by the data monocultures of their individual channel.

If you have outsourced your operations and supporting technology to vendors, your analytics go, too. No longer can you carry out what Forrester Research's Sean Corcoran calls CRAP (Collection, Reporting, Analysis, Prediction). And you aren't likely to get this information from the agency, either. Many agencies complain that clients don't want to pay for the Collection and Reporting end of the process, and most vendors don't want to reveal their proprietary Analysis and Prediction. The information they will send back to you is likely to be too summarized, selective, and superficial to be useful. In the end, by outsourcing analytics to vendors, you have hollowed out the thinking part of the marketing organization along with the doing part. Even if you have retained some product and channel managers, they will be so stretched that they will barely be able to execute operationally, much less think strategically about what they're doing.

Even if a request to hire someone for an analytically intensive job shakes free, these jobs take time to fill. Without a well-defined analytic approach and a culture of informed decision-making, a qualified analyst will bounce off your firm's atmosphere or end up in that no-man's land between marketing and IT, disconnected from the decisions they need to support and unable to use the firm's technology platforms to sense what's happening in the market.

Any advisor hired in these situations is going to under-achieve. I had coffee recently with an experienced analyst who had previously worked at a major multi-channel retailer. His job had been to build predictive models that would allow the retailer to better target different offers and promotions in direct marketing campaigns. Then he and his teammates left the retailer to build a small but successful firm to offer this same service for a range of clients. In his new role, he described for me a common frustration. He gets hired to build a predictive model for a client. "We find great opportunities," he said. "But when we show them to the client, the client just shrugs and says it looks great, but they can't do anything with it." The reasons vary. Sometimes it's that creative's swamped or IT is backed up. Sometimes they say it's too complicated to execute. Sometimes they say they've re-budgeted and can't afford to move on the idea. Other times they do get excited and still won't act. They say, "Cool! Let's get back to it after we clear what's on our plate. We can barely breathe right now."

The result is un-coordinated, un-differentiated customer experiences. Sound familiar?

Where To

By contrast, try to envision a beefed up, analytically-savvy product and channel marketing capability, one in which your people are regularly mining both owned and outsourced data sets for relevant, differentiated, and proprietary insights. They are working closely and productively with IT and external vendors to deploy no-more-complicated-than-necessary services to customers. To do that, they are working through a quickly iterated, permanent-beta-test process. In short, this is a high-performance, pragmalytic organization.

Recently, my kids were studying Eastern religions in school. This drawing was inspired by their studies as it helps to describe the behavioral sweet spot we're after. (Please contain your profound sense of awe.)

Figure 18: Profound Idea

Surely you will find other life-changing messages in it. Let me know if you do! Here are three points the picture suggests to me:

- You shouldn't waste your time or money developing insights you can't act on because you lack the capacity, or those you won't act on because you lack the inclination. Of course this can be a chicken-and-egg dilemma. As a practical matter you need to decide that you want an insight-driven process—or more of one—before looking for specific insights. Ordering insights à la carte and then failing to act on them will demoralize your staff and partners.

- On the flip side, common tropes call this the age of experimentation, and exhort us to adopt an action by default policy or to "Just Do It." They urge us not to fear failure. These are fine pieces of advice if your actions and experiments are based on clear logic and if you have set up an infrastructure to evaluate the results and take new actions based on what you've learned. Otherwise, there's no reason to charge ahead, because actions without clear feedback loops don't teach you anything. In fact it's hard to know if these actions are even effective.

- The choice to say *insight* rather than *data* or *analysis* is intentional. Your goal is to build a culture where you gather just enough data and analysis to develop an insight you can act on quickly and safely. This creates virtuous cycles that get you the support for more and more ambitious efforts.

How To

So you'd like to develop your organization in a pragmalytic direction:

- How do you evaluate and develop team members?
- How do you motivate them?
- How do you organize and support your analytic capability?

If you have already used the diagnostic for analytic decision-making suggested in the preceding chapter, you have a sense for where people are. How can you help them develop further?

Here's where you can begin to design and implement your development curriculum, based on the ideas presented earlier in this book. For the same reason that many leading business schools center on the case study method, you should focus your curriculum on real world opportunities. (This is how Force Five Partners works with clients. We develop capability to generate results through practice that builds confidence and helps pay the tuition.) So, the curriculum should start with:

- The best answers you got from anybody who responded to the challenge of improving revenues as described in Chapter Seven.
- Your own answers.
- Suggestions from colleagues and other advisors.

Where it's clear that certain team members need a primer, you can encourage them to develop their own version that blends references to outside resources with short, original work describing what's unique to your organization. For example, if you need to explain how cookies and tagging work in web analytics, you might combine references to generic guides with descriptions of your internal standards and practices. Don't forget a list of people who can help answer any questions.

Make your curriculum dynamic. Implement it in a way that allows commenting, tagging, aggregating feeds of this activity, and evaluation and access to people sources. Your firm may already have a collaboration tool for this, such as SharePoint, or Socialtext. If it doesn't, there are plenty of options.

Give people analytic sandboxes in which to experiment. Many people, if they use analytic tools at all, just stop with the canned reports the tools make available. If you create separate profiles for users, say, in your web analytics tools, you can let them experiment with custom reports, segments, and filters through which they can illuminate and vet insights and opportunities.

This brings us to motivation. Robert Schaffer and Harvey Thomson outlined what in my experience is the best theory for addressing motivation in their article "Successful Change Programs Begin with Results." The article appeared in the January, 1992 issue of *Harvard Business Review*, and it asserted that the first thing to do is to find one or two well-supported ideas that are simple enough to execute immediately. Then recognize the people behind them in visible ways. Be sure to recognize everyone who pitched in with contributions to each idea, in particular any IT folks who helped gather or manipulate data, or who helped assess the feasibility of a recommendation. What does it mean to recognize someone's contribution? Initially, it means packaging the success and the many people behind the success into a portable story that can be easily remembered and re-told. Then help the story to go viral with a celebration or two. As you see particular people involved in specifically useful ways recognized from multiple perspectives, you can allow recognition to extend to compensation, new opportunities, and promotions. Even as you sing songs about heroes and their mighty victories, however, remember to communicate the process and be transparent about the evaluation criteria for good opportunities and execution, to make them accessible and reproduce-able. Also remember to talk openly about efforts that didn't produce great results but did yield valuable lessons, and recognize folks involved with these as well. People will be watching closely the balance you strike here.

The Role of Analytic Specialists

OK, let's say you've got the people you have as practically developed and motivated as you can make them. Now the easy opportunities to translate this potential into results have begun to dwindle, and the ones you have left to develop cannot be easily developed through hypothesis-driven analytic approaches and tested with relatively little sweat. You'll know when you've hit this point because phrases like *cluster analysis*[17] are starting to come up in polite conversation. As they say in the oil business, it's time to re-pressurize the well. Now is a good time to bring in specialists.

When you bring in process or tool experts to accelerate your progress, don't let them take over your analytic process. Ideally, they should provide temporary scaffolding and ideas for making what you have better. Remember that your ends-focused staff can learn the means by learning SQL, statistics, or web programming. Make sure your team understands even grungy stuff such as tagging digital assets on pages, emails, posts in social media and coupon codes. Your people should know this well enough to keep a hand in, even if you choose to delegate 99 percent of it. You'd be surprised at how strategic some seemingly mundane choices can be at that level.

At the same time, we're in an era when you can blink and miss several revolutions. Just as we absorbed the conventional web, social media

---

[17]   http://en.wikipedia.org/wiki/Cluster_analysis_%28in_marketing%29

exploded. And now, just as we're wrapping our heads around social media, we have mobile going off in six different directions. Oh, have we covered e-readers and tablets? By staying ends-focused we keep from confusing a mobile strategy and all its accompanying tools with a strategy for targeting customers whose experiences prominently feature mobile devices.

A good way to spend some time would be to re-read parts of Avinash Kaushik's book, *Web Analytics: An Hour a Day*. In Chapter 15, "Creating a Data-Driven Culture—Practical Steps and Best Practices" Kaushik has some wonderful advice about the characteristics you want in a web analytics manager. It also details the relationship you want with outside help that I think extends well beyond web analytics. Kaushik is a true web analytics guru who was kind enough to get me into the Google Analytics beta program early on. One point on which my perspective differs from his—as I interpret it—is that I believe in pushing analytic capabilities more deeply and widely in the organization. Everyone has different skills, and each person should play to his or her strong suit, but I've observed that analytic fluency is pervasive in really high-performing organizations. I'm sure Kaushik would agree that the role of the web analytics team and especially its leader is to demystify and educate as much as it is to provide answers. But, as Lao-Tzu said, "When the best leader's work is done, the people say, 'We did it ourselves.'" And, as DIS Corporation founder Judah Phillips has written, it takes the whole organization to make good analytics happen.[18]

Speaking of organization, the first big decision is about the degree of centralization of decision-making in the business, and the analysis to support it. This is ultimately a function of strategic characteristics of the business. You want to ask broad questions. How high are the stakes involved in individual decisions? How predictable is the business environment? How reliably can you respond to this environment using automated rules tweaked from the center? You also need to consider how much development and discretion you invest in your people on the front lines. All else flows from this. If your answers to these questions are all

---

[18]   http://www.mediapost.com/publications/?fa=Articles. showArticle&art_aid=115611

"yes," you centralize a discrete brain trust. If they are all "no," you send coaches out to support the field.

Great, it's easy at the extremes. Where's the specific, practical middle for the centralization issue? First, it makes sense to me to centralize data governance. As Thomas Davenport and Jeanne Harris put it in their book *Competing On Analytics* (Harvard Business School Press, 2007), there needs to be one version of the truth. Also, logistically, it's safer and more efficient to collect and track data centrally. At minimum, you need to have a central registry where everything gets logged, even if in the most primitive fashion. Dark matter has no place in your data architecture. Second, you need to aggregate, document and share your standards and best practices with strong encouragement from the center. Also, you can source any specialized expertise from the center. Or, put another way, you should provide analytic support the way you'd provide support for technical APIs—if called properly, they are warranted to respond properly. Third, you should spread, delegate, or embed the actual analytic work into the business groups that use it. To help them, you might centralize a small but highly capable team to jump-start initiatives and coach the folks in different business groups. This also balances business intimacy with a breadth of perspective that helps drive innovation across the firm.

Another issue to be mindful of is that a team needs multiple skills to execute modern-day analysis. At minimum you may consider deploying people with complementary skills. For example you might pair a model-oriented business analyst with a data-oriented programmer who can marshal the necessary data from different sources to support the needs of a business unit. They may need additional help still from a unit-specific data or process analyst. In this case, the role of the center should be to identify and compensate for needed gaps.

Whether you go for a centralized or decentralized approach, the one thing we consistently see broken is the failure to involve IT as a business partner and then hold IT accountable as a partner from start to finish. I know of one example in which a retailer's marketing team had implemented a gift recommendation feature on its site. The feature used a third-party vendor's software-as-a-service parametric-search application, so that customers could theoretically narrow their search by selecting for several parameters including gender and age. In theory the items on the narrowed list should have been prioritized first through their popularity, then for a given range of popularity, they would further be sorted by their profitability for the firm. Instead, the sort order stayed true to its default settings, based on the calendar date the item was added to the product database. This was true regardless of whether any sale, let alone a profitable one, had ever been made. Root cause? The software-as-a-service vendor's Javascript code was tossed over to IT, and IT stuck it on the relevant pages with no questions asked of the marketers who wanted it, but hadn't thought about their configuration options. How was the problem identified? Someone noticed the suspiciously high bounce rates on the search results page, which were higher than bounce rates when customers used a method powered by a different search tool.

What's the moral of the story? Setting up a more pervasive *analytic marketer* approach to analytics is a catalyst for a conversation about business objectives, but it also helps find and fix problems as organizational friction reveals them. In fact, it can build bridges across organizations before the friction starts.

AFTERWORD

Book-writing tips are more or less like marketing advice. You have to know your audience, and you have to write what you know.

The hardest part of this project was staying calibrated to the intended reader, a pretty narrow band. If you are reading this, you are probably an accomplished senior executive, now a generalist who is good at balancing analytic rigor with creativity and practicality. You are curious enough about leaves and trees but focused on the forest, and you are skilled at both communication and execution.

These characteristics are what have brought you to your current responsibilities and they are fueling your momentum toward even more important achievements. But you've probably also come to understand that they make you pretty unique, and that it's difficult to initiate the change you want to see if you are working alone.

I hope that the knowledge I've shared has been useful to you, and I hope to have the chance to learn from you as well.

At minimum, then, this book is a request to start a conversation.

If you think you need help, vendors and advisors offer three choices. They can do it *for* you. They can do it *to* you. Or they can do it *with* you. If you're in the middle of a turnaround, and you and your management team are operating with a very short clock, the first option may make the most sense. We've played these roles with good results, but the capability development we strive for is harder under these conditions. If you have a very specific skill set or tool gap you are looking to fill, and you're confident you've got the right needs identified, the second path (do it *to* you) will be the most appropriate, because you can hire specific tools and training from a vendor. But if you are still feeling your way forward, in which you have an okay start but not yet good-enough performance, and you'd like to build an organization that can sustain and extend whatever initial progress you can spark, the third way might be for you.

If the ideas and experiences presented in this book seem appropriate for your firm and its goals, I welcome a chance to discuss your needs and our approach to see if we're a fit to work with you.

Regardless, thanks for taking the time to read Pragmalytics!

ABOUT THE AUTHOR

Cesar A. Brea is Managing Partner of Force Five Partners, LLC (http://forcefivepartners.com), a marketing analytics agency that works with clients in a number of industries to design and execute multi-channel marketing strategies and to build pragmatic, sustainable analytic foundations.

Cesar has more than 20 years' experience as a line executive, advisor, and entrepreneur. Prior to co-founding Force Five Partners, Cesar served as Global Practice Leader of Marketspace, Monitor Group's digital media and marketing advisory practice. Formerly, Cesar was CEO of Contact Networks, a web-based social networking service sold to Thomson Financial, and was SVP for Sales and Marketing at Razorfish, the interactive agency and systems integrator, through its acquisition by SBI. Before Razorfish, Cesar was VP for Marketing and Business Development at ArsDigita Corporation, an open-source software firm focused on online communities acquired by Red Hat. Earlier, he was a management consultant at Bain & Company and a banker with J.P. Morgan.

Cesar holds an MBA from Dartmouth's Amos Tuck School, where he was named an Edward Tuck Scholar, and received his undergraduate degree from Harvard College. He is a frequent writer and speaker on marketing in the digital age, and has served for many years as a judge in the Massachusetts Innovation and Technology Exchange's (MITX) interactive marketing and technology competitions. Cesar has been a guest lecturer in an advanced computer science course at MIT, as well as at Harvard's Kennedy School. He writes about marketing and e-business on his weblog at http://octavianworld.org.

Cesar lives in Dover, Massachusetts with his wife and three children.

APPENDIX

Analytic Brief Questionnaire

1: Which customers or groups are you targeting?

A: Segmentation either doesn't exist, or it exists but is documented only in research. (Weak)

B: Segmentation is integrated into our marketing plan, with clear ties between segments and campaign elements. (OK)

C: Segmentation is relevant and actionable for the marketing investment decision being made. It has also been integrated into reporting and analysis that is used to track and manage the marketing plan. (Good)

2: What do you know about how customers make buying decisions?

A: Relative influence of different channels is known generally, but in non-experiential fashion. (Weak)

B: The general customer experience is known. (OK)

C: Customer experience is known on a segment-by-segment basis. (Good)

3: More specifically, what do you know about which channels influence which segments?

A: We can cite general research, such as Pewinternet.org (Weak)

B: We can identify specific media within each channel, with specific data and examples. (OK)

C: We have specific data, and our examples have been integrated into personas (user portraits), use cases, and creative briefs for marketing campaigns. (Good)

4. How do you expect your target customers' habits to change?

A: Our marketing plans don't make any such projections. (Weak)

B: Our marketing plans incorporate assumptions from primary and secondary research. (OK)

C: Our marketing plans make appropriate room for testing and experimentation. (Good)

5. Which channels do you use? Which are you planning to use?

A: We can give a partial answer based on financial considerations. Ex. "We mostly use search; it gives us the best bang for our buck." (Weak)

B: We can give an answer that references our target customers. Ex. "The people we're trying to reach spend most of their time in channels x and y." (OK)

C: We can tell you how our marketing plans track customers, and to use this tracking ability to better integrate the customer's experience, in addition to simply reaching and converting customers affordably. (Good)

6. What role do you expect each channel to play?

A: We can give a non-quantified, channel-by-channel answer. (Weak)

B. Our marketing plan describes specific, quantified goals for each channel. These goals tie back to an overall model of the business. Ex. "If we want to put x on the top line, working backwards we need to do y through this channel." (OK)

C. We can describe specific, quantified goals for each channel and we can do so within the context of a desired experience for the target segment. (Good)

7. How effectively—and efficiently—does your current channel mix move people through their buying processes?

> A: We can offer an overall conversion rate and cost per order. (Weak)
> B: We can offer an overall conversion rate and cost per order on the basis of each customer or unique visitor. (OK)
> C: We can offer yield and cost by segment for each channel at each stage. (Good)

8. Where do folks get stuck or drop out? And why?

> A: We don't have data on that. We are purely focused on conversion. (Weak)
> B: We have data on the effectiveness of marketing in different channels, but little or no root-cause analysis. (OK)
> C: We can provide root-cause analysis for channels where this data can be collected, such as web properties, call centers. And our primary research (surveys, focus groups) is available for less measurable channels. (Good)

9. What information at each step would help you motivate and serve customers better?

> A: We use data only from each current channel to shape customer experience. (Weak)
> B: We have the ability to use data from prior interactions in other channels. (OK)
> C: We can supplement each step further with data available or purchased from third parties. Of course, we remain fully compliant with privacy policies and regulations. (Good)

FURTHER READING

Thinking, Fast and Slow by Daniel Kahneman (http://bit.ly/AgEU3U)

Supercrunchers by Ian Ayres (http://www.randomhouse.com/bantamdell/supercrunchers/)

Competing on Analytics: The new science of winning (www.amazon.com/Competing-Analytics-New-Science-Winning/dp/1422103323)

Web Analytics and *Web Analytics 2.0* by Avinash Kaushik (http://amzn.to/NbzxJj)

Web Analytics Demystified by Eric Petersen (http://amzn.to/LSglkt)

The Inmates Are Running the Asylum by Alan Cooper (http://www.cooper.com/journal/2003/08/the_origin_of_personas)

"How to Create a Customer Experience Framework" *CRM Magazine.* (http://www.destinationcrm.com/Articles/CRM-News/Daily-News/How-to-Create-a-Customer-Experience-Framework—57710.aspx)

Multichannel Marketing: Metrics and Methods by Akin Arikan (http://bit.ly/KWW74Z)

Multi-channel Attribution advice from Avinash Kaushik

(http://www.octavianworld.org/octavianworld/2012/07/wonderfully-pragmalytic-multi-channel)

INDEX